OLD MASTER DRAWINGS
FROM CHRIST CHURCH, OXFORD

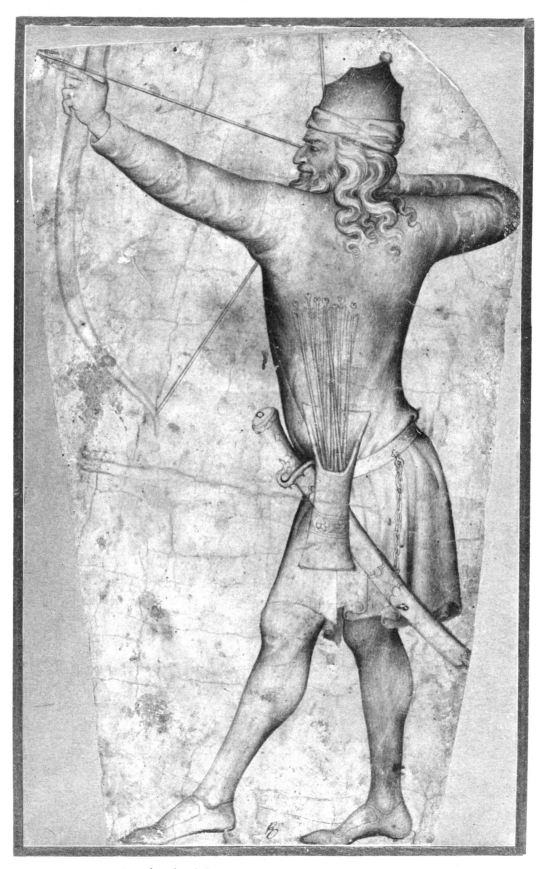

FRONTISPIECE: French School, late XIV century (Master of the Parement de Narbonne), *An Archer Drawing His Bow* (cat. no. 111)

OLD
MASTER DRAWINGS
FROM
CHRIST CHURCH
OXFORD

A LOAN EXHIBITION

INTRODUCTION AND CATALOGUE

BY JAMES BYAM SHAW

CIRCULATED BY THE

International Exhibitions Foundation

1972 – 1973

Participating Museums

NATIONAL GALLERY OF ART
WASHINGTON · D.C.

PHILADELPHIA MUSEUM OF ART
PHILADELPHIA · PENNSYLVANIA

THE PIERPONT MORGAN LIBRARY
NEW YORK · NEW YORK

THE CLEVELAND MUSEUM OF ART
CLEVELAND · OHIO

THE ST. LOUIS ART MUSEUM
ST. LOUIS · MISSOURI

*This project is supported by a grant from the National Endowment for the Arts
in Washington, D.C., a Federal agency*

COPYRIGHT © 1972 BY INTERNATIONAL EXHIBITIONS FOUNDATION
LIBRARY OF CONGRESS CATALOGUE CARD NO. 72-83826
PRODUCED BY THE MERIDEN GRAVURE COMPANY AND THE STINEHOUR PRESS

Cover Illustration: Cat. No. 84. Andrea del Verrocchio, *Head of a Young Woman*

Acknowledgments

CONTINUING its tradition of specializing in exhibitions of Old Master Drawings, the International Exhibitions Foundation is proud to present a group of drawings from one of England's most distinguished collections, that of Christ Church, Oxford.

The Pictures Committee and the Governing Body of this venerable college have generously agreed to lend more than one hundred magnificent examples for a tour of five museums starting with the National Gallery of Art in Washington, D.C. This selection includes rare works by many of the greatest draughtsmen of all times, and we are well aware how privileged we are to obtain this exceptional loan.

We are particularly indebted to Professor Humphrey Sutherland, Curator of Pictures, and to John Gordon-Christian, Assistant Curator, for making the loan arrangements, and we also wish to express our profound gratitude to the Dean of Christ Church, Dr. Henry Chadwick.

Our warmest thanks are due our old friend James Byam Shaw, who organized the exhibition and wrote the scholarly Introduction to the catalogue and the descriptions of the drawings, which contain a wealth of new information. This present catalogue precedes his major publication of the more than two thousand Christ Church drawings, which is nearing completion.

The International Exhibitions Foundation is grateful to the Ambassador of Great Britain, The Right Honourable the Earl of Cromer, for undertaking the sponsorship of the exhibition during its tour.

As always, the directors and trustees, as well as many staff members of the participating museums, have cooperated with us in every way to make the exhibition a success.

In addition, we owe special thanks to Harold Hugo and William J. Glick of The Meriden Gravure Company and C. Freeman Keith of The Stinehour Press for their invaluable assistance in the production of the catalogue.

We wish to note here how grateful we are to Mrs. Margaret Breitenbach for her assistance with the editing and proofreading of this catalogue, the thirtieth publication by the Foundation since 1966. Miss Heidi Droz, Mrs. Diana Swandby, and Miss Melba Myers of the Foundation staff contributed all their talents toward the efficient solution of the innumerable practical problems involved in the planning of this major exhibition.

ANNEMARIE H. POPE
President
International Exhibitions Foundation

Introduction

EVERY year hundreds of thousands of visitors—possibly more than half of them American—go through the gateway under the great tower built by Sir Christopher Wren into the most famous quadrangle in Oxford, familiarly called Tom Quad, the principal quadrangle of Christ Church, probably the best known (though not the oldest) of the Oxford colleges. Only the best informed of these visitors find their way to the new Picture Gallery, hidden behind the south side of the furthest quadrangle, called Canterbury; and probably not one in a thousand knows that it contains, besides some very important paintings, one of the finest collections of drawings by old masters in the whole of Britain. Perhaps this is not surprising, for there are other celebrated things to see at Christ Church which have been there a very long time—the Cathedral, the great Hall, the Library; and though the collection of drawings has belonged to the college since 1765, its installation in the new Picture Gallery is very recent. Even now, for reasons of conservation, the drawings cannot be displayed permanently. The exhibition in America of over a hundred of the best of them, arranged by the International Exhibitions Foundation with the consent of the Governing Body and the cooperation of Dr. Humphrey Sutherland, the present Curator of Pictures at Christ Church, is therefore a highly interesting event.

Even in England, only three large exhibitions of Christ Church drawings have ever been presented to the public. The first, as long ago as the winter of 1878–79, at the Grosvenor Gallery, London, is not likely to be remembered by anyone now alive; it consisted of ninety-one of what were then considered the most important specimens; and though no catalogue exists (so far as I know), forty-eight of the exhibited drawings were photographed at the time. The *Grosvenor Gallery Photographs* are recorded in Bell's *Christ Church Drawings*, published in 1914, and the references are given in the present catalogue for those drawings that are exhibited here. The second exhibition, of sixty drawings (and a few paintings), was held more than eighty years later at the Matthiesen Gallery, London, in 1960, in aid of the Christ Church charitable clubs, at the suggestion of Mr. John Synge, an old member of the college, and at that time a partner in the Matthiesen firm. The Matthiesen catalogue was made by Dr. Ursula Schmitt, with the help of other scholars; and it was used again, *verbatim*, for the third exhibition, at the Walker Art Gallery, Liverpool, in 1964, which showed somewhat fewer drawings, but included a much larger number of the Christ Church paintings.

Dr. Schmitt's was the first catalogue, properly so called, to be devoted exclusively to Christ Church drawings, although Sir Sidney Colvin had published many of the more important, along with many from the Ashmolean Museum, in his valuable portfolios entitled *Oxford Drawings* (finally dated 1907), and Sir Karl Parker included some in his catalogue of the exhibition *Disegni di Oxford* at the Fondazione Giorgio Cini in Venice in 1954. To say this implies no disrespect for C. F. Bell's publication of 1914 (now long out of print); for, as Bell himself was the first to admit, that was no more than an alphabetical handlist of the drawings then comprising the mounted series—rather more than 1100 out of nearly 2000 in all; its chief value lies in an admirable historical introduction and 125 small but good illustrations.

It is interesting evidence of the change of taste, and (I suppose I may say) advance of scholarship in certain fields of study, that no less than twenty of the drawings in the present exhibition were still unmounted until a few years ago, and therefore not included in Bell's handlist; and that Bell himself expressed the opinion in his introduction that the residue of unmounted drawings in 1914 included "nothing of importance and very little of any interest whatever." In 1964, when Dr. D. Bueno de Mesquita took over the curatorship, a programme of remounting and reboxing of the drawings was implemented, to coincide with the transfer of the collection from an upper floor of the Library to the new Picture Gallery, which was opened by H. M. the Queen in May 1968. The old mounts, made of pulp board at the end of the last century, had caused some damage to the drawings themselves. These were totally discarded, and new mounts were made, to enclose and reveal, in most cases, the XVII- or XVIII-century "mats," with their interesting if often fanciful ascriptions. More convenient solander cases replaced the heavy, battered leather boxes which older visitors to the collection will remember. At the same time the opportunity was taken, not only to dismount a number of relatively worthless specimens which had been included in the mounting programme of seventy years before, but also to mount for the first time a large number of interesting drawings, some of them indeed of great importance, which had been hitherto neglected. Examples of these latter in the present exhibition are: the splendid Pontormo study for the *Deposition* (no. 58), the fine figure study by Agostino Carracci (no. 13), Ludovico Carracci's *Ecce Homo* (no. 16), and Domenichino's *Flying Putto* (no. 24). Others will easily be identified from the present catalogue: they are recorded as "not in Bell."

Thus an early private collection of great interest and importance, one of the few remaining in England, has at last been rendered presentable and made fully available to the growing number of students of old master drawings. The selection now on loan to some of the great museums of the United States, where these studies are now so popular, includes only three of our five authenticated Leonardo drawings, only one of two Raphaels, and only two of Michelangelo, though two more have been recognized at Christ Church by recent authority; there are many more of Tintoretto in our boxes, and much else, in the series of some 1200 drawings that are now well mounted, of interest both to the student and the amateur, for which no room could be found in this exhibition. But it does include the three drawings that are, for my taste, the most beautiful of the whole collection: the late-XIV-century *Archer Drawing his Bow* (no. 111), the large and exquisitely finished Hugo van der Goes (no. 98), and the superb head attributed to Giovanni Bellini (no. 5). I must also draw attention to the fine representation here of the Florentine school of the XV–XVI centuries, from the time of Verrocchio (no. 84) to the time of Vasari, Empoli, and Cigoli; and also of the Bolognese and Roman schools of later date. That reflects in fact the character of the whole collection, in which the Northern schools, the Netherlandish and German for instance, are numerically much less strongly represented than the Italian. Nevertheless, a collection that includes such non-Italian drawings as are here exhibited—the Dürer, the de Gheyn, or Rubens' *Head of the Emperor Galba*, besides the XIV-century *Archer*, the Van der Goes, and an outstanding Ribera—cannot be reckoned negligible in this respect.

I have already written something of the origins of the Christ Church collection (basing my remarks on Bell's fundamental essay) in an issue of *Master Drawings* (VI, 3, 1968, pp. 235ff.), which was largely devoted to Christ Church drawings and included contributions by various colleagues, American and British. I need not repeat it all here. It was probably true to say that virtually nothing has been added to the collection of drawings since the bequest of General John Guise (1682–1765) of all his paintings and drawings to his old college in 1765. It was not true, however, to say (as I did then) that all the drawings in the present collection came from Guise, though the great majority did: we now know for certain that a few, at least, came from Henry Aldrich, who was Dean of Christ Church when John Guise took his degree in 1701, and who died in 1710. The two Barlow drawings, for example, in the present exhibition (nos. 114 and 115) belonged to him. The Dean was a great amateur of the arts, and it is very likely that his tastes were reflected to some extent in those of his pupil Guise.

Of the general himself, a brave soldier and a great "character" in his time, I have written at some length in the introduction to my catalogue, *Paintings by Old Masters at Christ Church, Oxford*, published by the Phaidon Press in 1967. Having taken his degree at Christ Church, and narrowly missed election to a fellowship of All Souls' College (as Mr. Ian Fisher has lately discovered), Guise joined the First (or Grenadier) Regiment of Foot Guards, and subsequently saw service and took part in some hard fighting in many parts of the world. Was it not an age of enlightenment, when two young professional soldiers, the future Duke of Devonshire and John Guise, who both served under Marlborough, spent their leisure in forming collections of the drawings of the old masters? Already in 1724 George Vertue refers to Guise in one of his notebooks as the owner of "a fine collection of drawings of the Italian Schools"; and to judge from certain examples which are apparently of the second half of the XVIII century, it seems likely that he continued to collect drawings (as he did paintings) to the end of his long life. We know something of his sources of supply, from the early collectors' marks and from other evidence; and it is noticeable that many of these are the same as those from which the 2nd Duke of Devonshire formed the chief part of the present collection at Chatsworth. The famous marks of Lanière, Lely, Lankrink, Richardson all appear—there are nearly fifty examples of Lely's mark at Christ Church; and no other collection except Chatsworth has so many drawings with the mark—the minute letters and numerals—of the Milanese antiquary Padre Sebastiano Resta, denoting that part of his immense holdings which came to England and was bought by John, Lord Somers about 1710, and sold at auction (after Somers' death) in 1717. There are over fifty examples from this collection at Christ Church—more than double the number recorded by Bell. Perhaps the Duke of Devonshire's judgment was more discriminating than Guise's; almost certainly he could afford to pay higher prices; but their tastes, and the scope of their collections, were similar, and they may sometimes have stood beside one another at Cocke's or Langford's in London, in the days when men of fashion frequented the auction-rooms in person and made their own bids. Visitors to the present exhibition, who also saw one or both of the Chatsworth exhibitions in the United States in 1962–63 and 1969–70, may be interested to compare samples of two collections that are nearly of the same age.

Guise also bought much abroad, in the intervals of his military service—according to the few early accounts of his activities, and to judge from the numerous inscriptions and attributions in foreign hands that occur on the old mats. Rome and Paris, one would guess, were his chief hunting grounds, when duty and the political situation allowed. One foreign dealer from whom he probably acquired a great deal—including almost certainly the two sheets from Vasari's famous *Libro di Disegni* (nos. 39 and 40 of the present catalogue)—was already named by C. F. Bell, though no one seems to have taken much notice of that interesting discovery: he was Salomon Gautier of Amsterdam and Paris, whose manuscript catalogue of an extensive collection, which was apparently in his hands for disposal in the early years of the XVIII century, is in the Bodleian Library at Oxford. Bell identified several of the Christ Church drawings as from this source, and I have identified a good many more—from the handwriting on the old mats, the type of the mats themselves, and the numbers written on the backs. That is the sort of evidence on which most of our researches into Guise's sources of supply must be based; and it is only from such evidence, probably, that it will be possible to draw any further conclusions about one more identifiable source of the Christ Church collection, the last that I need mention here: I mean the collection of the celebrated historian of Venetian art, Carlo Ridolfi (1594–1658), represented at Christ Church by a large number of drawings inscribed with the long straggling R (which is the Ridolfi mark, though certainly added after Carlo Ridolfi's death), often accompanied by an attribution (in what I call "the Ridolfi hand") that is surprisingly erratic for a historian of art (see no. 111 and others now exhibited). It would be tedious to enlarge here on the complicated problem presented by this part of the collection, which, if it was not quite certainly included in the Guise bequest, was certainly not acquired subsequently. I have written something on the subject in *Master Drawings* of 1968; and such further evidence as I have been able to muster must be delayed for publication in the complete catalogue of the drawings at Christ Church, which it is hoped will be published by the Oxford University Press before the end of 1973. The entries in the present catalogue are in most cases abbreviated from the entries made for that purpose.

It will be noticed, I hope, how often I am indebted for suggestions to colleagues in England, in America, and on the Continent of Europe. Their names are gratefully recorded in the text, and I will not repeat individual acknowledgments here. I must however make a special acknowledgment to Mr. John Gordon-Christian, the Assistant Curator of Pictures at Christ Church. The burden of mechanical work in the production of any catalogue is very tiresome, and most of this he has taken off my unequal shoulders; but much more important, ever since he came to Christ Church three years ago, his eye, his judgment and his memory have been invaluable to me in every aspect of my work on a long and difficult assignment.

J. BYAM SHAW

Mark of the CHRIST CHURCH collection (Lugt No. 2754). With a very few exceptions (see Introduction), all the Christ Church drawings appear to have come from the collection of General JOHN GUISE (1682/83–1765). A soldier who fought under Marlborough and later saw service in many parts of the world, Guise was a well-known connoisseur in his day, acting as artistic adviser to Frederick, Prince of Wales. On his death he left his large collection of paintings and drawings to Christ Church, from which he had taken his degree of B.A. in 1701. Guise himself used no collector's mark; the Christ Church mark has only been used since the end of the XIX century.

NICOLAS LANIÈRE or LANIER (1588–1666) (Lugt Nos. 2885 and 2886). Son of Queen Elizabeth's court musician, Lanière filled the same post under Charles I and as a connoisseur of prints and drawings made purchases for the Royal Collections. He also assisted Lord Arundel to form his collection. His two marks were for long confused with those of his patrons.

CARLO RIDOLFI (1594–1658) (Lugt Nos. 2175 and 2176). Historian of Venetian painting and biographer of Tintoretto. His drawings are generally marked with a long straggling R which seems, however, to have been added some time after his death. In addition they often bear on the old mounting paper inscriptions in an apparently earlier hand, *e.g.*:

Lionardo da Vinci m a (see No. 33).

SIR PETER LELY (1618–1680) (Lugt No. 2092). Lely came to England in 1641 with William, Prince of Orange, but reached the height of his fame as a portrait painter under Charles II. He bought largely at the sales following the dispersal of collections after the Civil War, and also paintings and drawings by Van Dyck from his widow. After his death his collections were sold to pay his debts in 1688 and 1694. Lely's collection was the first in England to be systematically stamped with a mark, this being affixed to his drawings by his executor Roger North before the sale of 1688. William Gibson (d. 1703), the miniature painter, was among those who bought at this sale (see Nos. 46, 54, and 56). Altogether more than fifty of Lely's drawings are at Christ Church.

PROSPER HENRY LANKRINK (1628–1692) (Lugt No. 2090). A German who studied in Antwerp and came to England where he was employed in the studio of Lely. He acted as auctioneer at the first Lely sale in 1688 and bought some of the drawings himself. He also acquired drawings from the collections of Charles I and Lord Arundel. His own collections were sold in London in 1693 and 1694.

P Resta (see No. 106). These small letters and numerals are the mark of at least part of the vast collection of drawings formed by the Milanese antiquary Padre SEBASTIANO RESTA (1635–1714) (Lugt No. 2992). Sixteen volumes from this collection were described in a letter from the architect John Talman to Dean Aldrich of Christ Church in 1710, and offered to him for sale (2111 drawings at about £500). Most of the drawings seem to have come to England, but Aldrich died in that year, and they were bought by JOHN, LORD SOMERS (1650–1716) (Lugt No. 2981), the Lord Chancellor. A manuscript catalogue of the collection, probably made by the Richardsons (see below) when the drawings were rematted for Lord Somers, is in the British Museum. Somers' prints and drawings were sold in 1717, the year after his death. Over fifty drawings from this collection have been identified at Christ Church. For an important article by A. E. Popham on Resta's collections, see *Old Master Drawings*, Vol. XI, June 1936.

JONATHAN RICHARDSON Senior (1665–1745) (Lugt Nos. 2183 and 2184). Portrait painter, writer on art, and one of the greatest of *marchands amateurs*. He amassed a vast collection; his sale after his death, held on 22nd January 1747 and seventeen following days (Cock), contained no less than 4749 drawings alone. His son Jonathan Richardson the Younger (1694–1771) was his close collaborator.

SALOMON GAUTIER (Lugt Nos. 2977 and 2978 and Suppl. p. 419). Dealer in Amsterdam and Paris in the early XVIII century. A sale of his paintings and prints took place in London (Howard) 10th March 1717. Many of the Christ Church drawings, no doubt sold by Gautier to General Guise, can be identified in a manuscript catalogue of his large collection of drawings now in the Bodleian Library, Oxford.

EXHIBITIONS

Royal Academy, London, 1927, *Flemish and Belgian Art 1300–1900*.

Royal Academy, London, 1930, *Italian Art 1200–1900*.

Royal Academy, London, 1938, *17th Century Art in Europe*.

Royal Academy, London, 1949, *Landscape in French Art 1550–1900*.

Royal Academy, London, 1953, *Drawings by Old Masters* (Diploma Galleries). Catalogue by K. T. Parker and J. Byam Shaw.

Royal Academy, London, 1960, *Italian Art and Britain*.

The Matthiesen Gallery, London, April–June 1960, *Paintings and Drawings from Christ Church, Oxford*.

Newcastle, Department of Fine Art, King's College, 1961, *The Carracci: Drawings and Paintings*. Catalogue by Ralph Holland.

Walker Art Gallery, Liverpool, 1964, *Masterpieces from Christ Church: The Drawings*.

Catalogue

NOTE ON THE CATALOGUE The entries for the drawings and, in most cases, the illustrations, have been arranged alphabetically under artists within the two major divisions, the Italian School and the Non-Italian Schools. The Non-Italian Schools have been subdivided into five schools. Where there is more than one drawing by the same artist, the drawings are arranged in the order of the Christ Church inventory numbers. Height precedes width in the measurements.

ABBREVIATIONS

Bell   C. F. Bell, *Drawings by the Old Masters in the Library of Christ Church, Oxford*. Oxford, 1914.

Passavant   J. D. Passavant, *Tour of a German Artist in England* (English ed.). 2 vols., 1836. The Christ Church collection is described in Vol. II, pp. 131–140.

Waagen   Waagen, *Treasures of Art in Great Britain*. 3 vols., London, 1854, with Supplement. The Christ Church collection is described in Vol. III, p. 47.

Robinson   J. C. Robinson, *A Critical Account of the Drawings by Michel Angelo and Raffaello in the University Galleries, Oxford*. Oxford, 1870.

Colvin   Sidney Colvin, *Selected Drawings from Old Masters in the University Galleries and in the Library at Christ Church, Oxford*. 6 vols., Oxford, finally dated 1907.

Grosvenor   Photographic facsimiles of forty-eight of the Christ Church drawings,
Gallery   selected from an exhibition of ninety-one drawings held at the Gros-
Photographs   venor Gallery, London, 1878–79.

Popham   A. E. Popham, *Italian Drawings Exhibited at the Royal Academy, London, 1930*. Oxford, 1931. A complete illustrated record.

Catalogue

I · ITALIAN SCHOOL

Niccolò dell'Abate (?)
c. 1509–1571

1 DESIGN FOR A DECORATIVE PANEL OR WALL-MONU-MENT, WITH TWO PUTTI SUPPORTING A BLANK MEDALLION ABOVE, AND ALLEGORICAL FIGURES SEATED BELOW (0182)

Pen and brush and dark brown wash, heightened with white body color, on blue prepared paper.

412×275 mm.; 16×10¹³⁄₁₆ in.

Inscribed in Padre Resta's hand: *Primo stile Parmeggianinesco di Nicolo dell'Abbate.*

Provenance: Padre Sebastiano Resta; John, Lord Somers (*K.85*); General John Guise.

Literature: Bell, E.30.

Resta's attribution of this impressive draw-ing to Niccolò is disputed by Mr. John Gere, who considers it too clumsy for an artist whose best known work is distinguished for its elegance of form and execution. He also draws attention to the dependance of the composition on part of Perino del Vaga's decoration of the Sala della Giustizia in the Castel S. Angelo in Rome, which so far as we know Niccolò never saw, and which cannot be earlier than 1540/41. There is an elaborate drawing by Perino for this part of the composition in the Royal collection at Windsor Castle (Popham-Wilde, cat., 1949, No. 979 and Pl. 73), and it might be argued that Niccolò could have seen that; but in any case Gere's remarks cannot be disregarded, and the old attribution must be treated with reserve.

On the other hand, we know very little about the earliest stages of Niccolò's artistic career, and since he seems likely not to have started it at a very early age (for he is said to have been a soldier), it is perhaps possible that he drew in this rather coarser style in the first half of the 1540s, when, as Padre Resta's inscription says, he was imitating Parmigianino, and was probably also influenced by the brothers Dossi. The Christ Church draw-ing could be some years earlier than Nic-colò's frescoes from Palazzo Torfanini, now in the Pinacoteca of Bologna (*c.* 1548–50) and the concert-scenes of Palazzo Poggi (now part of Bologna University) (*c.* 1550–52); and in both of these works there are considerable points of resemblance. Niccolò departed to France in 1552, and from then onwards his style becomes increasingly man-nered and elegant.

The inscription *Coreggio* on the rim of the medallion is in Richardson's hand. Mr. Hugh Macandrew has pointed out that this space was formerly filled by another drawing, similarly inscribed, which is now mounted separately at Christ Church (inv. no. 0400).

It is a pretty drawing of the *Virgin and Child*, perhaps by Bernardino Gatti or Giorgio Gandini.

Alessandro Algardi
1595–1654

2 DESIGN FOR AN ALTAR (?)
(0905)
Pen and light brown wash over rough black chalk.
262 × 197 mm.; 10⁵⁄₁₆ × 7³⁄₄ in.
Provenance: General John Guise.
Literature: Bell, BB.21; W. Vitzthum in *Bollettino d'Arte*, 1963, p. 86, Fig. 22.

The purpose of this charming design is not clear, and is not discussed by Dr. Vitzthum in his publication.

Baccio Bandinelli (?)
1493–1560

3 A CAMEL
On the *verso* (visible through the backing), another study of the same animal from the front   (0093)
Red chalk.
232 × 301 mm.; 9¹⁄₈ × 11⁷⁄₈ in.
Provenance: General John Guise.
Literature: Bell, C.12 (as attributed to Bandinelli); Christopher Lloyd in *Burlington Magazine*, 1969, p. 374 and Fig. 51.

The attribution to Bandinelli, first made perhaps by J. C. Robinson or Colvin, is supported by Mr. Pouncey and accepted by Mr. Lloyd. There are animal drawings in red chalk by Bandinelli in the Louvre (see *Art Quarterly*, XVIII, 1955, Figs. 16 and 17); and one of an ox in the Uffizi was at the Royal Academy Italian Exhibition in 1930 (repr. Popham, *Italian Drawings*, 1931, Pl.

CCII, No. 239). I am not absolutely convinced that the hand is the same, in spite of a superficial resemblance.

Jacopo da Ponte, called Bassano
1510/15–1592

4 DIANA IN THE CLOUDS
(1341)
Black chalk on blue paper, heightened with white.
508 × 379 mm.; 20 × 14¹⁵⁄₁₆ in.
Provenance: Sir P. Lely (L.2092); General John Guise.
Literature: Not in Bell; A. Ballarin in *Arte Veneta*, XXIII, 1969, p. 107 and Fig. 121.

Though not included either by Arslan or by H. and E. Tietze, this is by far the best of the drawings by or attributed to Bassano at Christ Church, exceptional in size and quality, and as a subject very unusual in the artist's *oeuvre*. It might represent the goddess appearing at the Sacrifice of Iphigenia.

Attributed to Giovanni Bellini
c. 1430–1516

5 BUST OF A MAN, WEARING A CAP AND AN EMBROIDERED COAT; perhaps the portrait of Gentile Bellini, the artist's brother (0263)
Black chalk, washed over, on paper originally white.
391 × 280 mm.; 15⁵⁄₁₆ × 11 in. (top corners cut).
Provenance: General John Guise.
Literature: Bell, H.9 (as Alvise Vivarini); Berenson, *Lorenzo Lotto*, 1901, p. 92 (as

Alvise Vivarini); Colvin, II, 32 (Alvise Vivarini); G. F. Hill, *Portrait Medals of Italian Artists*, 1912, Pl. 3; J. Byam Shaw in *Old Master Drawings*, II, 1928, p. 54 (probably Giovanni Bellini); A. E. Popham, *Italian Drawings at the Royal Academy, 1930* (1931), No. 177 (perhaps by Bonsignori); H. and E. Tietze, *Drawings of the Venetian Painters*, 1944, p. 88, No. A.318 (Mantegna); W. Suida in *Art in America*, 1946, p. 63 (Mantegna); L. Dussler, *Giovanni Bellini*, 1949, p. 84 (perhaps Mantegna); E. Tietze-Conrat, *Mantegna*, 1955 (Mantegna); F. Heinemann, *Giovanni Bellini e i Belliniani*, 1959, p. 224, v.48 (as by Gentile Bellini); V. N. Gratchenkov, *North Italian Portrait Drawings of the late Quattrocento*, in *Essays in Honour of Victor Lasarev* (in Russian), Moscow, 1960, pp. 266–268 (Giovanni Bellini); Ursula Schmitt in *Münchner Jahrbuch*, 1961, p. 139, No. 105 (Giovanni Bellini); Gratchenkov, *Drawings of the Italian Renaissance*, Moscow, 1963, Pl. 1 (Giovanni Bellini); Felton Gibbons in *Art Bulletin*, 1963, p. 56 (Giovanni Bellini); M. Lanckorońska, *Neithart in Italien*, 1967, pp. 60–61 (as the portrait of Mantegna by Grünewald).
Exhibited: Royal Academy, 1930, No. 620; Royal Academy, 1953, No. 40; Venice, 1958, Fondazione Giorgio Cini, *Disegni Veneti di Oxford*, No. 2; Matthiesen, 1960, No. 3; Mantua, 1961, Mantegna Exhibition, No. 131; Liverpool, 1964, No. 1.

I have cited in this instance a very full bibliography, in order to emphasize the variety of opinions expressed as to the authorship of this splendid drawing.

The identification of the man portrayed as Gentile Bellini, first proposed by Colvin and G. F. Hill, has been supported recently by Professor Felton Gibbons (*loc. cit.*) with reference not only to the portrait-medal of Gentile by Camelio, but also to that by Gambello, and to various paintings and drawings. His comparisons seem to me convincing: the long nose, flaring out at the tip, with the strongly marked nostril, is particularly characteristic. The letters *IM. NV* on the coat have been supposed to be a German motto, and as such inappropriate to Gentile Bellini; but it seems unlikely that the sitter was a German, and if he was Italian, Gentile, who was created a knight and then a count by the Emperor Frederick III, is as likely as any other to have worn a ceremonial coat with a German motto. In any case it seems to me more probable that the four letters *IM. NV* are only part of a longer inscription, partly concealed by the fold in the coat and partly cut off by the edge of the paper.

If the man portrayed is Gentile Bellini, it is surely unlikely that a member of the Vivarini family, the chief rivals of the Bellini in Venice, should have had either the wish or the opportunity to portray him. And I suspect that neither Alvise Vivarini nor Francesco Bonsignori—both artists of the second rank—was capable of producing so fine a head as this. To be dogmatic in a case where opinions are so divided would be very unwise; but my feeling is that the choice of attribution lies between Giovanni Bellini (drawing his brother) and Mantegna (drawing his brother-in-law), and that the minor claimants can be excluded. If the drawing of Francesco Gonzaga in the Dublin Gallery, which I attributed (*loc. cit.*) more than forty years ago to Giovanni Bellini, is really by

Mantegna, as some believe, then the Christ Church drawing must be by him too, for they are surely by the same hand. But there is nothing really comparable among drawings certainly by Mantegna, as Erika Tietze admitted; and the few independent painted portraits by him—*Cardinal Mezzarota* in Berlin, or *Cardinal Carlo de' Medici* in Florence—severely linear, almost wooden in effect—do not convey that sense of structural unity in the neck and head to which I have already drawn attention in the two drawings at Christ Church and in Dublin. This structural unity is consistently characteristic of portrait-paintings that are either signed by or plausibly attributed to Giovanni Bellini: I refer to such as the so-called *Colleoni* in Washington, the *Young Man* in the Capitoline Gallery, Rome, or the double portrait formerly in the collection of Lord Kinnaird (Berenson, *Venetian Lists*, 1957, Pl. 254).

The date of the drawing may be *c.* 1495, when Gentile was about sixty-five or sixty-six.

Ascribed to
Gian Lorenzo Bernini
1598–1680

6   HEAD OF A YOUNG MAN
WEARING A CAP   (0614)
Red chalk, slightly heightened with white, on buff paper.
249 × 194 mm.; 9¹³⁄₁₆ × 7⅝ in.
Provenance: General John Guise.
Literature: Bell, s.1.

The attribution of this excellent drawing derives from two XVII-century inscriptions on the *verso*, visible through the backing: *Cavalier Bernini* and *Sig:ʳᵉ Bernini*. The latter is

repeated in an early XVIII-century hand on the back of the Richardson-type mat. The model might have been an apprentice in a sculptor's studio wearing a paper cap (such as Michelangelo is said to have worn) to keep the dust out of his hair.

Professor A. S. Harris (from a photograph) will not accept the attribution, and it is true that the use of red chalk only (with a very little white), instead of the red and black more usual in Bernini's drawn portraits, results in a certain flatness and lack of plasticity here. But I am not entirely convinced by her objections; the treatment of the hair seems characteristic; and I prefer not to disregard a near-contemporary ascription, especially when the work in question is not the sort of thing for which the artist was best known to his contemporaries.

Andrea Boscoli
1550–1606

7   A STAG-HUNT; IN A RENAIS-
SANCE FRAME, WITH A
PORTRAIT HELD BY A
PUTTO ABOVE: Design for
a wall panel   (0933)
Pen and brown wash and watercolor.
182 × 138 mm.; 7³⁄₁₆ × 5⁷⁄₁₆ in.
Provenance: Guillaume Hubert (L.Suppl. 1160); General John Guise.
Literature: Bell, cc.11 (as Italian School, 1600–1650).

Mr. Popham suggested that this charming drawing may have been inspired by the great hunting-scene designed by Federico Zuccaro in 1565, as the back-cloth for a comedy performed in Palazzo Vecchio, Florence, on the occasion of the marriage of Francesco de' Medici to Giovanna of Austria. Zuccaro's vast drawing, in watercolor and tempera, is now in the Uffizi. Boscoli's drawing seems certainly to show something of Zuccaro's influence.

Giacinto Brandi
1623–1691

8 S. PETER NOLASCO (?) INTERCEDING WITH THE VIRGIN FOR TWO CAPTIVES (1254)
Pen and brown and grey wash over rough black chalk, heightened with white body color, on grey paper. Squared in black chalk for enlargement.
537 × 268 mm.; 21⅛ × 10 9/16 in.
Provenance: General John Guise.
Literature: Not in Bell.

Both Mr. Jacob Bean and the late Dr. Walter Vitzthum expressed the view that the old attribution of this fine drawing to Giacinto Brandi should not be lightly discarded, even though the comparison with drawings in the Louvre, which bear old ascriptions to him, is not completely convincing. Brandi was Lanfranco's pupil in Rome, and something of Lanfranco's influence is traceable here.

The subject is obscure, but St. Peter Nolasco, who was canonized in 1628, nearly four centuries after his death, was venerated as the co-founder of the Order of Mercy for the Redemption of Christian Prisoners.

Angelo Bronzino
1503–1572

9 THE VIRTUES AND BLESSINGS OF MATRIMONY EXPELLING THE VICES AND ILLS (1340)

Black chalk and very pale brown wash. Squared for enlargement.
399 × 308 mm.; 15 11/16 × 12⅛ in.
Provenance: General John Guise.
Literature: Not in Bell; E. Pillsbury in *Report and Studies in the History of Art*, Washington, National Gallery, 1970, pp. 74–83; Catherine Monbeig-Goguel, *Il Manierismo Fiorentino*, 1971, p. 89 and Fig. 10.

This important late drawing by Bronzino was identified by Mr. E. Pillsbury (in November 1969) as the working drawing for one of a set of five vast paintings, dedicated to the theme of Matrimony, which were ordered to decorate the façade of Palazzo Ricasoli, by the Ponte alla Carraia in Florence, on the occasion of the marriage of Francesco de' Medici and Giovanna of Austria in December 1565. Three of them were designed by Bronzino and two by Allori. The drawing for another of the series, *The Preparation of the Marriage Bed*, also by Bronzino (but, unlike the present drawing, outlined with the pen) is in the Louvre (Voss, *Malerei der Spätrenaissance*, 1920, Pl. 71; Pillsbury, *loc. cit.*, p. 78 and Fig. 5). The programme for the series (in which the subject of the Christ Church drawing is given as *Il Discacciamento del Male*) was devised by the humanist Vincenzio Borghini, whose letter to Duke Cosimo, the bridegroom's father, dated April 5, 1565, is quoted by Venturi, IX, 6, p. 15. See Vasari, ed. Milanesi, VII, p. 604, and P. Ginori Conti, *L'Apparato per le Nozze di Francesco de' Medici e di Giovanna d'Austria*, Florence, 1936, pp. 17–20.

Domenico Campagnola
1500–1564

10 MOUNTAIN LANDSCAPE

WITH A FORTRESS; A YOUNG GOATHERD AND HIS DOG IN FOREGROUND RIGHT (0318)

Pen and brown ink. Indented with the stilus.

243 × 388 mm.; 9⁹⁄₁₆ × 15¼ in.

Provenance: Sir P. Lely (L.2092); General John Guise.

Literature: Bell, I.21; Colvin, II, 36; Tietze, 1944, p. 130, No. 527 (with a wrong reference to Bell, I.22).

Exhibited: Venice, Fondazione Giorgio Cini, 1958, *Disegni Veneti di Oxford*, No. 13.

H. and E. Tietze call this fine drawing "late, shop." Sir Karl Parker (catalogue of the Venice exhibition, 1958) considers it certainly by the master, though not of the first quality. I should say that of its type it is a very good example. The buildings in the background, it is true, seem to be collapsing towards the right, but that fault is characteristic of Campagnola's distances, at least in his later drawings, and the boy and the animals in the foreground are particularly well drawn. Certainly this is the best of the interesting series of landscapes by him from the Lely Collection at Christ Church. Only three of them are mentioned by H. and E. Tietze.

The whole of the landscape is repeated in the reverse direction, without the figures and with a different sky, in another Christ Church drawing, inv. no. 0319.

Simone Cantarini
1612–1648

11 THE VIRGIN AND CHILD, SEATED (0555)

Red chalk.

272 × 210 mm.; 10¹¹⁄₁₆ × 8¼ in.

Provenance: General John Guise.

Literature: Bell, Q.13.

A particularly characteristic and charming example.

Vittore Carpaccio
c. 1460/65–c. 1525

12 BUST OF A YOUNG MAN IN A CAP, TOWARDS LEFT (0282)

Black chalk, brush, and a little pale brown wash on blue paper, heightened with white body color.

265 × 187 mm.; 10⁷⁄₁₆ × 7³⁄₈ in.

Provenance: Padre Resta; John, Lord Somers (not numbered, but identifiable); General John Guise.

Literature: Bell, H.26; C. Ricci in *Rassegna d'Arte*, V, 1905, p. 77; Colvin, II, 33; D. von Hadeln, *Venezianische Zeichnungen des Quattrocento*, 1925, p. 60 and Pl. 15; A. E. Popham, *Italian Drawings at the Royal Academy*, 1930 (1931), No. 171; G. Fiocco, *Carpaccio*, 1931, Pl. LXIX, and *Carpaccio*, 1958, p. 35; Van Marle, XVIII, 1936, p. 330; H. and E. Tietze, 1944, No. 629 and Pl. XVI. 1; J. Lauts, *Carpaccio*, 1962, p. 275, No. 41 and Pl. 64; T. Pignatti in *Master Drawings*, I, 1963, p. 50; P. Zampetti, *Carpaccio*, 1966, p. 22; T. Pignatti, *La Scuola Veneta (I Disegni dei Maestri)*, 1970, p. 82 and Pl. VII.

Exhibited: Royal Academy, 1930, No. 690; Venice, Fondazione Giorgio Cini, 1958, *Disegni Veneti di Oxford*, No. 5; Matthiesen, 1960, No. 8; Royal Academy, 1960, No. 522; Stockholm, *Konstens Venedig*, 1962–63; Liverpool, 1964, No. 5.

This fine drawing, often exhibited and highly praised, is generally thought to be of the period of the paintings for the Scuola di S. Orsola in Venice, now in the Accademia. It may safely be dated 1495–1500. Corrado Ricci's attempt to identify the man with one of the bystanders in the *Preaching of St. Stephen* (1514), now in the Brera, Milan, is not convincing.

Agostino Carracci
1557–1602

13 A WARRIOR SUBDUING A MONSTER (1355)
Black chalk and light brown wash, squared in red chalk. All corners cut and made up.
548 × 388 mm.; 21 9/16 × 15 3/16 in.
Provenance: General John Guise.
Literature: Not in Bell; J. Byam Shaw in *Master Drawings*, VI, 1968, pp. 255–257 and Pl. 18.

This fine drawing, published for the first time in 1968, may be a preliminary idea by Agostino for one of the grisaille "terminal" groups of warriors subduing harpies, which divide the main subjects in the series of frescoes in the Sala di Enea of the Palazzo Fava, Bologna. All three Carracci are generally supposed to have taken part in the decoration of this room, but their respective shares, and the date, have been much disputed. I am inclined to agree with Dr. G. C. Cavalli (*Mostra dei Carracci*, 1956, cat. p. 74) in supposing that the Sala di Enea was decorated *c.* 1593–94, and that this is the date of the Christ Church drawing. I have given my reasons for believing that the drawing is much more characteristic of Agostino in style than of either his cousin Ludovico or his brother Annibale; and that is the attribu-

tion written in an early XVIII-century hand on the old mounting-paper.

14 ANCHISES: STUDY FOR THE FRESCO *ANCHISES AND VENUS* IN THE GALLERIA FARNESE, ROME (0471)
Pen and brown ink over red chalk.
370 × 255 mm.; 14 9/16 × 10 1/16 in.
Provenance: General John Guise.
Literature: Bell, 0.6.

No notice has so far been taken in the Carracci literature of this important drawing, which in my opinion is rightly attributed (in a XVII-century hand on the backing) to Agostino, but is clearly a preliminary study for a fresco always supposed to have been painted by his brother Annibale. There are significant differences between the drawing and the painting: in the latter there is drapery across the lap of Anchises, and he wears Roman sandals on both feet; the position of Venus' right leg is different; and Anchises in the fresco is removing not a stocking but a laced sandal from her foot. In the fresco, too, the facial type of Anchises is heavier, older-looking; and the background accessories are differently disposed. Our drawing is not a copy, but a preliminary study from the nude model—the leg of Venus being no doubt a makeshift invention of the artist.

The modelling of the body with the pen, with hatchings and cross-hatchings following the form of the muscles in the style of an engraver, is more characteristic of Agostino than of Annibale. The *Anchises and Venus* in the Farnese ceiling is in the immediate neighborhood of the fresco of *Cephalus and Aurora*, one of the two large subjects known to have been finished by Agostino before he departed from Rome in 1600 (before June); and as there is reason to believe that the whole of the ceiling may have been finished by this time, it may well be that Agostino had at least planned (and prepared drawings for) some of the neighboring scenes as well. If the fresco of *Anchises and Venus* was executed by Annibale, then we may suppose that he made use of some of his brother's material. No one has ever suggested that Agostino painted this fresco himself, and it is true that the early writers limit his participation to the two larger frescoes to which I have referred; but the type of Venus here, and the cool greyish flesh-color, struck me when I last visited the Farnese Gallery as closer to those of Agostino's *Cephalus and Aurora* and *Glaucus and Scylla* than to the more florid types and warmer, reddish flesh-tones of (let us say) Annibale's *Triumph of Bacchus and Ariadne*.

Annibale Carracci
1560–1609

15 A MALE NUDE SEATED TOWARDS RIGHT, RIGHT ARM BEHIND BACK (0502)
Red chalk, with some white.
416×245 mm.; 16³⁄₈×9⁵⁄₈ in.
Provenance: Padre Resta; John, Lord Somers (*e.46*); General John Guise.
Literature: Bell, P.1 (as attributed to "Carracci").
Exhibited: Newcastle, 1961, No. 67 (as by Annibale Carracci).

Figures in somewhat similar poses appear *en grisaille* in that part of the ceiling of the Camerino Farnese that originally enclosed the central subject of *Hercules at the Crossroads* (this canvas now in Naples; Martin, *The Farnese Gallery*, 1965, Figs. 5–8). But nearly all identified drawings for the Cam-

erino are in black chalk, and in some respects the Christ Church drawing is closer to one of the caryatids painted in greenish bronze below the fresco of *The Combat of Perseus and Phineus* in the Galleria (see particularly Martin, Fig. 81). These figures were certainly not painted by Annibale's own hand (Bellori says they are partly by Domenichino), but I see no reason not to attribute this fine drawing to the master himself.

Ludovico Carracci
1555–1619

16 CHRIST SHOWN TO THE PEOPLE (1158)
Pen and brown wash, over red chalk.
335×370 mm.; 13³⁄₁₆×14⁹⁄₁₆ in.
Provenance: General John Guise.
Literature: Not in Bell.

This drawing, hitherto unpublished and never exhibited except at Christ Church, must be one of the final studies for Ludovico's fresco of the *Ecce Homo*, painted (according to Bodmer) *c.* 1595, in the portico of Palazzo Ercolani in Via Galliera, Bologna, but later transferred to the Oratorio di S. Filippo Neri, which is now incorporated in the church of the Madonna di Galliera (Bodmer, *Lodovico Carracci*, 1939, Fig. 37). The fresco in its present state is rectangular above, showing less of Pilate's canopy, and ends immediately to the right of the man holding up the robe of Christ; there are other variations, but in general the correspondence is close.

An earlier stage in the development of the composition is represented by another drawing at Christ Church, inv. no. 1624, inscribed as a copy after Ludovico (presumably after a drawing) by his pupil Francesco

Brizio. In this Pilate is placed on the right. A further sketch for the whole scene by Ludovico himself, again with Pilate on the right, belongs to Dr. Robin Adair, New York (from the collection of Sir Joshua Reynolds, and correctly identified in an inscription in Reynolds' hand).

Ludovico's composition, particularly in the earlier manifestations to which I have referred, seems to have been inspired by the *Ecce Homo* of Correggio's follower G. M. F. Rondani in the Cappella Centoni of Parma cathedral (repr. Popham, *Correggio's Drawings*, 1957, p. 103), which Ludovico must surely have seen when he visited Parma as a young man.

Ludovico Cardi, called Cigoli
1559–1613

17 STUDIES FOR TWO
CELESTIAL VIRTUES (0232)
Black and red chalk, heightened with white, on blue paper.
390 × 265 mm.; 15⅜ × 10⁷⁄₁₆ in.
Provenance: General John Guise.
Literature: Bell, G.12 (as attributed to Cristofano Allori); Jacob Bean in *Master Drawings*, VI, 1968, p. 259 and Pl. 26.

Mr. Bean (*loc. cit.*) identified this fine drawing as a study for two of the three celestial virtues inspiring St. Jerome in his study, in the altarpiece, signed and dated 1599, in the Church of S. Giovanni de' Fiorentini, Rome (Cappella di S. Girolamo). Several thumbnail sketches for the whole composition appear on the *verso* of a drawing in the Uffizi, No. 1030F.

18 *Recto*: A SOLDIER ON HANDS
AND KNEES, BLOWING UP

A FIRE (?)
Verso: TWO SOLDIERS
STANDING (1941)
Recto in black and a little red chalk, heightened with white body color, on grey-blue paper; *verso* in black chalk only.
250 × 407 mm.; 9⅞ × 16 in.
Provenance: Ridolfi (?); General John Guise.
Literature: Not in Bell.

Technique and paper would be quite characteristic of Cigoli, and the style is near to that of the *Two Celestial Virtues* (No. 17). Both sides might be studies for a *Martyrdom of St. Lawrence*, but Cigoli is not known to have painted that subject.

Jacopo Confortini
Working in Florence, early XVII century

19 CHRIST IN THE HOUSE OF
SIMON (1157)
Black chalk.
242 × 347 mm.; 9½ × 11¹¹⁄₁₆ in.
Provenance: General John Guise.
Literature: Not in Bell; Christel and Günther Thiem in *Mitteilungen des Kunsthistorischen Institutes in Florenz*, XI, November 1964, pp. 153ff.

A composition-study for one of the frescoes in the refectory of S. Trinità, Florence. The painting is signed by Confortini and dated 1630.

Little was known of Confortini until Dr. and Frau Dr. Thiem discovered his signature on two of the frescoes in S. Trinità, the commission for which was given to Giovanni da San Giovanni, but in which Jacopo Confortini was known to have participated. With these two frescoes the Thiems connected (*op. cit.*) a considerable number of drawings —including two complete composition-studies (at Christ Church and Hamburg), and several individual figure-studies for the same. For *Christ in the House of Simon*, the single figure-studies are at Coburg, in the British Museum (2), and at Edinburgh (Thiem, Figs. 9–12), and a drapery-study for the Magdalen is on the back of a sheet in Rome (*ibid.*, Fig. 6). Mr. Philip Pouncey, who had independently noted several of these drawings as Confortini's (on the basis of an inscription on a drawing in the Pierpont Morgan Library), has since observed that a study for the Christ in the same fresco has been repeatedly exhibited and reproduced in recent years as by Velásquez (Lopéz-Rey, 1963, Pl. 60).

The types and proportions of the figures in the frescoes signed by Confortini seem strangely robust compared to those in most of the drawings: and it could be argued that the two composition-studies, at least, might be the work of the presiding artist, Giovanni da San Giovanni—to whom in fact both of them were once attributed. The whole group of drawings, however, is so consistent in style that it would be difficult to suppose them by more than one hand; and the simple conclusion must be that the author of the frescoes is also the author of the drawings.

Since Dr. and Frau Thiem published their discovery, several other drawings by Confortini have been identified, including two more at Christ Church.

Correggio (Antonio Allegri)
c. 1490–1534

20 THE VIRGIN AND CHILD
     WITH SAINTS AND ANGELS
     (0387)

Point of the brush and brown color, over red chalk (washed over).
207 × 152 mm.; 8⅛ × 6 in.
Provenance: General John Guise.
Literature: Bell, M.1; G. Frizzoni in *L'Arte*, IX, 1906, p. 250; Colvin, II, 26; G. Gronau, *Correggio (Klassiker der Kunst)*, 1907, p. xli; C. Ricci, *Correggio*, 1930, p. 172; A. E. Popham, *Correggio's Drawings*, 1957, pp. 86 and 164, No. 75. Exhibited: Parma, Correggio Exhibition, 1935, No. 7; Matthiesen, 1960, No. 12.

The drawing is listed by Bell as a study for Correggio's *Madonna of St. George*, now in Dresden (before 1530), but all other authorities have connected it with the *Madonna of St. Jerome*, now in the Parma Gallery, commissioned in 1523, finished perhaps four years later, and always assumed to be the earlier of these two great altarpieces. The connection is not very close with either painting, but that with the *Madonna of St. Jerome* seems certain; for (as Mr. Cecil Gould suggested to me) the figure on the extreme right is surely a second thought for St. Jerome, who already appears more to the left in the same drawing, and was to be transferred in the final solution to the extreme left of the composition—leaving space on the right to be filled by the figure of St. Catherine. On the other hand the smaller figure on the left of the Christ Church drawing seems more nearly related in pose to the youthful Baptist in the *Madonna of St. George*, with his left foot on the step of the throne. He is, however, not a youthful Baptist; he is surely an angel, holding a large open book (not a bowl, as Popham interpreted it); and this brings us back to the *Madonna of St. Jerome*, where in the painting an angel, standing in front of St. Jerome, is presenting just such a volume (no doubt St. Jerome's Bible) to the infant Christ, who now turns in his direction.

It may be best therefore to describe the drawing not as a study, but as a confusion of half-realized ideas for the composition of an altarpiece, put onto paper soon after 1523 when Correggio first began to think about his commission to paint the *Madonna of St. Jerome*, some of which ideas lingered at the back of his mind when he came to paint the *Madonna of St. George* a few years later. Mr. Gould remarks that Correggio was economical with his ideas, and did not like to waste one, even if he had discarded it.

An unpublished drawing by Correggio in the Accademia, Venice (No. 521, attr. to Parmigianino), seems to represent a further stage in the evolution of the theme.

Pietro da Cortona
1596–1669

21 DESIGN FOR A WALL-DECORATION (0973)
Pen and brown wash over black chalk.
320×274 mm.; 12⅝ × 10¹³⁄₁₆ in.
Inscribed in the hand of Padre Resta:
Pietro da Cortona. Galleria di Mᵗᵉ Cavallo di Alessᵒ VII.
Provenance: Padre Sebastiano Resta; John, Lord Somers (*d.124*); General John Guise.
Literature: Bell, DD.7; Norbert Wibiral in *Bollettino d'Arte*, XLV, 1960, p. 140 (as by G. F. Grimaldi); G. Briganti, *Pietro da Cortona*, 1962, p. 310.
Exhibited: Royal Academy, 1938, No. 426; London, Wildenstein, 1955, *Artists in 17th Century Rome*, No. 33; Matthie-

sen, 1960, No. 13; Liverpool, 1964, No. 9.

Resta's inscription gives perfectly correct information: the drawing is a preparatory study by Cortona for the decoration of one of the walls in the so-called Gallery of Alexander VII in the Quirinal Palace in Rome. The commission was given to a group of artists under the direction of Pietro da Cortona by the Chigi pope soon after his accession, and executed 1656–57. Dr. Wibiral (*loc. cit.*) has given a valuable account of this important project; but he is certainly wrong in attributing the Christ Church drawing to Grimaldi. The latter took part in the decoration, but his style as a draughtsman is quite different. The drawing is in fact entirely characteristic of Cortona's hand, whether the painting for which it was intended (which has not survived) was executed by him or by one of his assistants.

Lorenzo Costa
c. 1460–1535

22 CHRIST IN THE HOUSE OF SIMON THE PHARISEE (0300)
Pen and brown ink.
296×453 mm.; 11⅝ × 17¹³⁄₁₆ in. (arched top).
Provenance: General John Guise.
Literature: Bell, I.4; C. Ricci in *Rassegna d'Arte*, V, 1905, p. 77; Colvin, II, 23.
Exhibited: Royal Academy, 1953, No. 35; Matthiesen, 1960, No. 14; Liverpool, 1964, No. 10.

Justly described by Colvin as the most important extant drawing of the master, the attribution of which has never been disputed. It is almost certainly to be dated after 1500.

Lorenzo di Credi
1457–1537

23 DAVID WITH THE HEAD OF GOLIATH AT HIS FEET (0057)
Silverpoint, heightened with white, on prepared ground.
280 × 126 mm.; 11 × 4 15/16 in.
Provenance: Padre Resta; John, Lord Somers (*g.95*); General John Guise.
Literature: Bell, B.11 (as School of Credi); Passavant, *Tour*, ii, 138; Berenson 995 (as Granacci); Colvin, I, 12 (the same); G. Dalli Regoli, *Lorenzo di Credi*, 1966, p. 109, No. 23 and Fig. 35.

A very early drawing by Credi, perhaps *c.* 1480, and of the finest quality though considerably damaged. The figure must have been inspired both by the bronze David of Donatello (the general pose) and by Verrocchio's bronze of *c.* 1475 (the left hand, and the turn of head and shoulders). The drawing is in fact extremely Verrocchiesque in style.

Domenico Zampieri, called Domenichino
1581–1641

24 A FLYING PUTTO CARRYING A STAFF AND AN APPLE: a cartoon (1381)
Black chalk, on four pieces of buff paper joined. Some contours indented with the stilus (pouncing irrelevant to the drawing). Top corners cut.
770 × 447 mm.; 30 5/16 × 17 11/16 in.

Provenance: General John Guise.
Literature: Not in Bell; Catherine Johnston in *Revue de l'Art*, VIII, 1970, pp. 56–59 and Fig. 5; the same, *Il Seicento e Settecento a Bologna* (*I Disegni dei Maestri*), 1971, p. 84 and Pl. XIX.

Formerly attributed to Cignani, but recognized by Miss Johnston as the cartoon for the closely corresponding figure at one end of the ceiling-fresco (*The Chariot of Apollo*) in Palazzo Costaguti, Rome. Sir John Pope-Hennessy has identified nine smaller drawings connected with the same work at Windsor (*Drawings of Domenichino*, 1948, Nos. 1053–1061), including one for the same putto.

The ceiling is to be dated *c.* 1615.

Jacopo da Empoli
1551–1640

25 A YOUNG MAN STANDING, IN CONTEMPORARY DRESS, POINTING WITH HIS RIGHT HAND (0562)
On the *verso* (visible through the backing), is a study of a nude figure in a similar pose, but with the right hand down to his side.
Red chalk.
411 × 225 mm.; 16 3/16 × 8 7/8 in.
Provenance: General John Guise.
Literature: Bell, Q.20 (as by Cavedone).

Mr. Pouncey's attribution to Empoli is clearly correct. The study seems in fact to have been used for the angel in Empoli's altarpiece of the *Annunciation* in S. Trinità, Florence (the first altar on the left). The artist evidently made the drawing from a *garzone* in the studio, and then indicated, with a few flourishing lines, how the angel's drapery should go.

Paolo Farinati
1524–1606

26 APOLLO IN HIS CHARIOT:
Design for a ceiling (1394)
Pen and brown ink, and brush and
brown wash, over black chalk on grey-
blue paper, heightened with white body
color. Octagonal.
440×420 mm.; 17$\frac{5}{16}$×16$\frac{9}{16}$ in.
Provenance: Sir P. Lely (L.2092); General John Guise.
Literature: Not in Bell.

One of the most important of Farinati's surviving drawings, so many of which belonged, like this one, to Sir Peter Lely.

Domenico Fetti
c. 1589–1623

27 BUST PORTRAIT OF CAT-
ERINA DE' MEDICI, WIFE
OF DUKE FERDINANDO I
OF MANTUA (0449)
Red and black chalks.
322×241 mm.; 12$\frac{11}{16}$×9$\frac{1}{2}$ in.
Inscribed on the *verso*, in a contempo-
rary hand: *Quest' è l'Effigie di Madama
Ser* ^{ma} *di Mantova / Moglie del Ser* ^{mo}
S ^{r} *Duca Ferdinando di mano d Domenico
Fettis.*
Provenance: General John Guise.
Literature: Bell, N.17^A; T. Pignatti in
Pittura del Seicento a Venezia, 1959, cat.
Disegni, No. 25.
Exhibited: Royal Academy, 1938, No.
446; Venice, 1959, *Seicento a Venezia*,
Disegni, No. 25; Matthiesen Gallery,
1960, No. 20.

Caterina de' Medici (1593–1629), daughter
of the Grand Duke Ferdinando I of Florence,

married Ferdinando Gonzaga, 1st Duke
(from December 1612) of Mantua, as his
second wife, in 1617. The drawing is probably to be dated before the death of the Duke
in 1626; but at that date the Duchess was
only thirty-three, and to judge from her appearance she cannot have been much younger
than that when the portrait was drawn.

It has been suggested that the Christ
Church drawing is by Ottavio Leoni, but it
is on a much larger scale than Leoni's portraits, and is obviously different in style. In
view of the uncertainty surrounding the attribution of drawings to Fetti it would be
rash in this case to contradict the circumstan-
tial inscription, in contemporary handwriting, on the *verso*. It is possible that Fetti, who
was brought up in Rome and was younger
than Leoni, was to some extent influenced
by Leoni's work; but that he was an eminent
portraitist in his own right is proved by the
Mantua Inventory of 1627, which records
twenty-three portraits by him in the ducal
collection. Furthermore, the influence of the
early work of Rubens, which Fetti must
have known in Mantua, is strikingly apparent here.

Giorgione (?)
c. 1477–1510

28 AN OLD MAN SEATED
WITH A BOOK UNDER HIS
ARM (0739)
Red chalk, rubbed over.
151×112 mm.; 5$\frac{15}{16}$×4$\frac{3}{8}$ in.
Provenance: General John Guise.
Literature: Bell, w.3^A (as Italian School,
1600–1650); Terisio Pignatti, *Gior-
gione* [1970], p. 106, No. 20 and Pl. 98
(much enlarged).

The drawing, which had escaped notice at Christ Church until a few years ago, seems obviously Giorgionesque, related in type to the St. Joseph both in the "Benson" *Holy Family* (now in Washington) and in the National Gallery *Adoration of the Magi*; but I should have hesitated to attribute it to the master himself, as Pignatti does (*loc. cit.*, relating it rather to the Vienna *Philosophers*). There are undeniable weaknesses, particularly in the drawing of the hands. On the other hand we have little in the way of standards for the appraisal of Giorgione's drawings: this does not look like a copy, and the one drawing that is generally accepted as authentic, the *Pastoral Scene with a View of Castelfranco* in Rotterdam (Pignatti, Pl. 53), is not incompatible in style, and hardly superior in quality.

Giulio Romano
1499(?)–1546

29 DESIGN FOR A GOLD GIRDLE, WITH A HUMAN MASK, SNAKES, ACAN-THUS, AND LION TER-MINALS; with one of the terminals repeated, and a rough sketch of the Gonzaga eagle (0853)
Pen and brown wash, over light black chalk. On four pieces of paper, joined.
265 × 378 mm.; 10⁷⁄₁₆ × 14⁷⁄₈ in.
Inscribed in a contemporary hand: *Cinta d'oro fatta al Sᵣ Vincentio guerin* (= Querini?).
Provenance: General John Guise.
Literature: Bell, AA.5; Hartt, 1958, No. 127 and Fig. 148.

Hartt misreads the name of Giulio's patron as Guerieri. The drawing is laid down, but

there seem to be some free sketches (an eagle with wings spread?) on the *verso*.

There is a large collection of ornament drawings by Giulio Romano at Christ Church, many of them silhouetted like those in the British Museum.

Giovanni Francesco Barbieri, called Guercino
1591–1666

30 A WOMAN, RICHLY DRESSED (ESTHER), SWOONING IN THE ARMS OF ANOTHER, half-length figures (0579)
Pen and brown ink.
188 × 156 mm.; 7³⁄₈ × 6¹⁄₈ in.
Provenance: General John Guise.
Literature: Bell, R.2.

The subject was rightly interpreted by Bell as *Esther swooning before Ahasuerus*. Mr. Mahon has observed that the drawing is a study for the painting now in the Ann Arbor Museum of the University of Michigan. According to Malvasia (*Felsina Pittrice*, 1841 ed., II, pp. 264, 291, 319) this was commissioned by Antonio Barberini, Cardinal of S. Onofrio, as a present for his brother, Pope Urban VIII, in 1639.

Giovanni Lanfranco
1582–1647

31 HEAD OF A YOUNG MAN LOOKING DOWN TO RIGHT (0540)
(At top right, and apparently drawn over the head-study, is a study of a left hand on a much smaller scale.)
Black chalk, slightly heightened with white chalk, on pale buff paper.

274 × 234 mm.; 10$\frac{13}{16}$ × 9$\frac{3}{16}$ in.
Provenance: J. Richardson sen. (L.2184); General John Guise.
Literature: Bell, Q.3.

A particularly sensitive study from the model. I cannot find that it was used in any of Lanfranco's paintings.

Giovanni Battista Lenardi

1656–1704

32 THE MARTYRDOM OF THE *QUATTRO CORONATI* (0611)
Pen and brown wash over red and black chalk, heightened with white body color, on brown toned paper.
477 × 356 mm.; 18$\frac{13}{16}$ × 14 in.
Provenance: General John Guise.
Literature: Bell, R.28.

Lenardi's drawings, to judge from signed or traditionally ascribed examples in the Royal Library at Windsor and in the collection of the Earl of Leicester at Holkham (Nos. 32 and 57[a]), might be described as tame Cortonesque, with rather heavy-handed contours; the present drawing, on the other hand, which is of exceptional size, is very freely drawn and extremely dramatic in composition, action, and lighting. The style has something of Cortona and perhaps something of Salvator Rosa, and the technique recalls that of Passeri. If this is by Lenardi—and the attribution goes back at least as far as the early XVIII century—it is by far the most impressive of such drawings as are known to me.

The *Quattro Coronati*, to whom a famous church in Rome is dedicated, were four Roman soldiers, Saints Severus, Severianus, Carpophorus, and Vittorinus, who refused to worship a statue of Aesculapius.

Leonardo da Vinci

1452–1519

33 STUDY OF A SLEEVE, AND PART OF A FACE (0036)
Pen and brown ink; the fragment of hair and cheek on the right in red chalk (but the eye in pen and ink).
81 × 94 mm.; 3$\frac{3}{16}$ × 3$\frac{11}{16}$ in.
Provenance: Ridolfi; General John Guise.
Literature: Bell, A.31; Berenson 1054; Colvin I, 14; Venturi, IX, i (1925), p. 63; A. E. Popp, *Leonardo Zeichnungen*, 1928, No. 4; Degenhart, *Rivista d'Arte*, XIV, 1932, pp. 440ff.; Calvi, *Raccolta Vinciana*, XIV, 1930–34, pp. 201–239; Bodmer, 1931, Pl. 110 (wrongly stated to be in the University Galleries); *Commissione Vinciana*, I, 11; K. Clark, *Leonardo da Vinci*, 1939, p. 14; Popham, No. 8[A].
Exhibited: Royal Academy, *Leonardo*, 1952, No. 17; Matthiesen, 1960, No. 36; Liverpool, 1964, No. 24.

This small drawing is of great importance, since it is clearly the study used for the sleeve of the angel in the Uffizi *Annunciation*, and provides proof that the Uffizi painting, which some critics have supposed to be by Verrocchio, is in fact by Leonardo and one of his earliest, to be dated *c.* 1472.

I see no reason to suppose (as Bodmer and Anny E. Popp did) that the fragment of a head in red chalk at the right margin is not by Leonardo himself at this early date; it is left-handed, and might even be a first idea for the head of the Virgin in the same painting.

34 *Recto*: TWO ALLEGORIES OF ENVY; WITH TWO INSCRIPTIONS IN LEONARDO'S HAND

Verso: TWO ALLEGORIES: (a) INGRATITUDE, ENVY, AND DEATH; (b) PLEASURE AND PAIN; WITH FOUR INSCRIPTIONS IN LEONARDO'S HAND (0034)

Pen and brown ink, with some light red chalk on the *recto*.

210×289 mm.; 8¼×11⅜ in.

Provenance: General John Guise.

Literature: Bell, A.29; Passavant, *Tour*, II, 136; Berenson 1051; Colvin I, 18, 19; Richter, *Literary Works of Leonardo*, Pls. LIX and LXI; Bodmer, 1931, pp. 158–159 (wrongly stated to be in the University Galleries); Commissione Vinciana, 99–100; McCurdy, *Notebooks of Leonardo da Vinci*, 1939, II, pp. 492–493; Popham, 1946, Nos. 107–108; Carlo Pedretti in *Burlington Magazine*, XCVI, 1954, pp. 175–178; the same, *Studi Vinciani*, 1957, pp. 54–61.

Exhibited: Royal Academy, *Leonardo*, 1952, No. 55; Matthiesen, 1960, No. 38; Liverpool, 1964, No. 21.

Professor Pedretti first drew attention to the fact that this and another allegorical drawing at Christ Church (inv. no. 0037) are those described, with their inscriptions paraphrased, by the Milanese artist Gian Paolo Lomazzo in his *Trattato dell'arte della Pittura*, Milan, 1584, pp. 449–451. Lomazzo must certainly have seen the Christ Church drawings and copied Leonardo's inscriptions.

In the center of the *recto* is represented Envy, in the form of a hag wearing a mask, riding on a skeleton representing Death.

This is explained by Leonardo in the note of twenty-one lines on the left: "This Envy is represented making a contemptuous gesture towards heaven, because if she could she would use her strength against God. She is made with a mask upon her face of fair appearance. She is made wounded in the eye by palm and olive. She is made wounded in the ear by laurel and myrtle, to signify that victory and truth offend her. She is made with many lightnings issuing forth from her, to denote her evil speaking. She is made lean and wizened because she is ever wasting in perpetual desire. She is made with a fiery serpent gnawing at her heart. She is given a quiver with tongues for arrows, because with the tongue she often offends; and she is made with a leopard's skin, since the leopard from envy slays the lion by guile. She is given a vase in her hand, full of flowers, and beneath these filled with scorpions and toads and other venomous things. She is made riding upon death because envy never dying has lordship over him; and death is made with a bridle in his mouth and laden with various weapons, since these are all the instruments of death" (translation from E. MacCurdy, *Notebooks of Leonardo*, 1938, II, p. 492).

On the right of the same side, a figure with two bodies growing out of one pair of legs is sufficiently explained by the note in four lines below: "In the moment when virtue is born she gives birth to envy against herself, and a body shall sooner exist without a shadow than virtue without envy" (*ibidem*). The latter part of this inscription is repeated on the *verso* of another drawing at Christ Church (inv. no. 0037), over another Allegory of Envy.

On the *verso*, to the right, is a figure with

two heads (one old, one young) and four arms, representing Pleasure and Pain. This is explained in the four lines above and the shorter inscription below: "Pleasure and Pain are represented as twins, as though they were joined together, for there is never the one without the other; and they turn their backs because they are contrary to each other." "If you shall choose pleasure, know that he has behind him one who will deal out to you tribulation and repentance."

A longer explanation of the same sketch is in the inscription at upper left: "This is Pleasure together with Pain, and they are represented as twins because the one is never separated from the other. They are made with their backs turned to each other because they are contrary the one to the other. They are made growing out of the same trunk because they have one and the same foundation, for the foundation of pleasure is labour with pain, and the foundations of pain are vain and lascivious pleasures. And accordingly it is represented here with a reed in the right hand, which is useless and without strength, and the wounds made with it are poisoned. In Tuscany reeds are put to support beds, to signify that here occur vain dreams, and here is consumed a great part of life; here is squandered much useful time, namely that of the morning when the mind is composed and refreshed; and the body therefore is fitted to resume new labours. There also are taken many vain pleasures, both with the mind imagining impossible things, and with the body taking those pleasures which are often the cause of the failing of life; so that for this the reed is held as representing such foundations."

Under this is a drawing of two naked figures (Malice and Envy) riding upon a monstrous frog, followed by Death with scythe and hourglass. The two figures are identified below as: "*il mal pensieri e invidia ov(ver)o ingratitudine.*" In the passage from Lomazzo, quoted by Pedretti (*loc. cit.*), there is a more detailed explanation of this, evidently paraphrased from a lost sheet of Leonardo's own.

All the inscriptions, as usual with Leonardo, are written from right to left and may easily be read with the aid of a looking glass.

Pedretti dates the drawing 1485–87.

35 GROTESQUE BUST OF A MAN IN PROFILE TO RIGHT (0033)
Black chalk, the contours pricked for transfer. Top corners cut.
382 × 275 mm.; 15 1/16 × 10 13/16 in.
Provenance: Giorgio Vasari (?) (the ascription to Leonardo on the left is in lettering that resembles his); General John Guise.
Literature: Bell, A.28; Colvin, I, 21; Berenson 1050; Bodmer, 1931 (*Klassiker der Kunst*), Pl. 305 (wrongly stated to be in the University Galleries); Popham, *The Drawings of Leonardo da Vinci*, 1946, No. 146; L. H. Heydenreich, *Leonardo*, 1954, Pl. 50.
Exhibited: Royal Academy, 1952, *Leonardo*, No. 88; Montreal, *Five Centuries of Drawings*, 1953, No. 36; Matthiesen, 1960, No. 40; Liverpool, 1964, No. 22.

Generally dated 1503–04, and plausibly identified by Berenson with a black chalk head described by Vasari: "*quella di Scaramuccia capitano de' Zingani, che poi ebbe Messer Donato Valdambrini d'Arezzo, canonico di S. Lorenzo, lassatagli dal Giambullari*" (ed. Milanesi, IV, pp. 26–27).

That the drawing has been retouched,

along the contours of the profile (with the brush ?) and on the cheek (with right-handed shading), has often been noticed and is undeniable. Perhaps the face was rubbed and damaged by frequent use of the drawing as a cartoon by Leonardo's pupils. The pricking is much closer along the retouched contours of the profile than it is on the neck and shoulder and round the head; the internal lines of the hair do not seem to be pricked at all. In spite of the damage, the drawing retains an effect of extraordinary vigor; and in the hair, the neck, and the shoulder, where there is little or no restoration, the touch of the master is evident.

Follower of Leonardo da Vinci
Late xv century

36   STUDY OF DRAPERY FOR A FIGURE KNEELING TOWARDS RIGHT   (0048)
Metal-point and white on grey-blue ground, with some brown wash.
251 × 187 mm.; $9\frac{7}{8} \times 7\frac{3}{8}$ in.
Provenance: Ridolfi; General John Guise.
Literature: Bell, B.2; Grosvenor Gallery Photographs, No. 6.

As Sir Sidney Colvin rightly observed (in a note on the mount), this beautiful drawing seems to be by the same hand as one in the British Museum (Popham-Pouncey, No. 127 and Pl. CXIV) which is a study for the drapery of the risen Christ in the Leonardesque *Resurrection* in Berlin (No. 90^{B}). Both drawings are demonstrably right-handed, and neither can be by Leonardo himself; but that at Christ Church, particularly, is of very high quality indeed; and it is nearly related in style to those studies of

drapery that Leonardo made (so Vasari tells us) by soaking linen in wet plaster and allowing it to set.

To judge by the indication of the figure, it may have been intended for a St. Jerome, or some other saint kneeling in adoration. But the drapery was certainly not arranged on a human model; it seems to be laid over a sort of stepped platform, with one corner propped up by some other means.

Jacopo Ligozzi
1547–1626

37   DANTE WATCHING THE SUNRISE IN THE DARK FOREST (*Inferno*, I, 16–18)   (0233)
Pen and brown wash, heightened with white body color, on brown tinted paper.
201 × 275 mm.; $7\frac{15}{16} \times 10\frac{13}{16}$ in.
Signed and dated below center: *iacopo Ligozzi invētor 1587*, and inscribed with the name of Dante.
Provenance: General John Guise.
Literature: Bell, G.13; B. Degenhart, *Die Illustrationen zum Dante*, in *Römisches Jahrbuch für Kunstwissenschaft*, VII, 1955; W. R. Jeudwine in *Apollo*, April 1959, p. 115, Fig. III; Robert McGrath in *Master Drawings*, V, 1967, pp. 31ff. and Pl. 18.
Exhibited: Amsterdam, 1955, *Le Triomphe du Maniérisme Européen*, No. 211; Matthiesen, 1960, No. 42; Liverpool, 1964, No. 26; Venice, 1971, Fondazione Giorgio Cini, *Disegni Veronesi del Cinquecento*, No. 103.

This and No. 38, together with one other at Christ Church and one in the Albertina, . form a group of illustrations to Dante that was evidently intended for engraving (to judge from the indentation of two of the three Christ Church drawings) and apparently produced at Mantua (to judge from the artist's inscriptions on one of those at Christ Church and the one in the Albertina). All are signed and dated 1587 or 1588. It is possible that a complete series was intended to be engraved and dedicated to the Duke of Mantua.

Mr. McGrath (*loc. cit.*) draws attention to the interesting fact that both Federico Zuccaro and Stradanus produced drawings to illustrate Dante at the same time as Ligozzi.

38 DANTE SURROUNDED BY THE THREE BEASTS, AND VIRGIL APPEARING TO DANTE (*Inferno*, I, 31ff.) (0234)

Pen and brown wash, heightened with white body color, on brown tinted paper. Indented with the stilus for engraving.

205 × 278 mm.; 8⅟₁₆ × 10¹⁵⁄₁₆ in.
Signed and dated lower left: *iacopo Ligozzi inventore 1587*, and inscribed with the names of Dante and Virgil.
Provenance: General John Guise.
Literature: Bell, G.14; Robert McGrath in *Master Drawings*, V, 1967, pp. 31ff. and Pl. 19.
Exhibited: Matthiesen, 1960, No. 43; Venice, 1971, Fondazione Giorgio Cini, *Disegni Veronesi del Cinquecento*, No. 104.

No engraving is known, but it seems likely from the indentation of this drawing that one was intended. See note to No. 37.

Filippino Lippi
1457–1504

39 A PAGE FROM VASARI'S *LIBRO DI DISEGNI*: Figure studies on two sheets, drawn front and back, in a *passe-partout* decorated on both sides by Vasari himself

Recto, above: the drapery of an angel, and three draped figures (that on the right on a separate piece of paper)
Recto, below: two draped, and two nude figures (that on the right on a separate piece of paper)
Verso, above: four nude figures, and a man's head (the nude on the left on the separate piece of paper)
Verso, below: two draped, and one nude figure, and a left ear (the draped figure on the left on the separate piece of paper) (1339)
Silverpoint, heightened with white, on slate blue ground.
Size of the whole sheet, including Vasari's *passe-partout*, 565 × 450 mm.; 22¼ × 17¹¹⁄₁₆ in. Upper row: 207 × 415 mm.; 8⅛ × 16⁵⁄₁₆ in. Lower row: 207 × 408 mm.; 8⅛ × 16⅟₁₆ in.
Inscribed on the *passe-partout* below, *recto*: *Filippo Lippi Pittor' Fior:* and *verso*: *FILIPPO LIPPI P:* probably by Vasari.
Provenance: Giorgio Vasari; General John Guise.
Literature: Bell, p. 63; Passavant, *Tour*, ii, 138; Colvin, I, 6–7; Berenson 853[A] and 1355[B]; *Old Master Drawings*, XII, 1937, Pl. 6 (*rectos* only).

These excellent figure-studies are characteristic of Filippino in his early, Botticellian manner, probably before 1480.

Lord Crawford pointed out to me that the draped figure on the left of the lower sheet *verso* nearly corresponds with the figure on the extreme right of Botticelli's *Adoration of* the *Magi* in the Uffizi. This is often supposed to be the artist's self-portrait (*Kl.d.K.*, *Botticelli*, p. 21) and the painting certainly belongs to the period when Filippino was working in Botticelli's studio, *c.* 1472–75. He was already described as an independent painter, and might perhaps have been responsible for the figure in question.

Berenson's entries (ed. 1961) are confusing, for he makes no mention of the Vasari provenance, and describes the two *recto* sides under one number (1355B) as by Filippino, and the two *verso* under another (853A) as by Davide Ghirlandaio. In fact *recto* and *verso* in each case are obviously by the same hand.

40 A PAGE FROM VASARI'S *LIBRO DI DISEGNI* (1338)

Recto: Two larger drawings (A,B) and three smaller (C,D,E), laid down on the sheet, with a woodcut portrait of the artist washed by hand; the drawings divided and surrounded by a decorative border by Vasari.

Verso: Another drawing, laid down on the back of the sheet, similarly enclosed in a framework by Vasari.

Whole sheet, 597 × 465 mm.; 23½ × 18 5/16 in.

Recto: A The Virgin and Child with Saints adoring: independent sketches of *putti* and angels above.
Pen and brown wash over black chalk.
286 × 198 mm.; 11¼ × 7 13/16 in.

B Sketches for the Afflictions of Job.
Pen and brown ink, with body color, over black chalk, outlines closely pricked for transfer.
291 × 206 mm.; 11½ × 8⅛ in.
Inscribed lower left: *dony* (?), apparently by the artist.

C A Man fighting a Centauress, and another carrying a slab of stone.
Pen and brown wash, irregular.
133 × 146 mm.; 5¼ × 5¾ in. (max.)

D A Centaur, a Woman, a Satyr, and Satyress, fighting.
Pen and brown wash, irregular.
136 × 157 mm.; 5⅜ × 6 3/16 in. (max.)

E Two Tritons carrying Trophies.
Pen and brown wash over black chalk, irregular.
86 × 104 mm.; 3⅜ × 4⅛ in. (max.)

Verso: Design for an Altarpiece dedicated to St. Nicholas of Bari, ascribed to *Altura Mantovano*.
Pen and light brown wash.
343 × 248 mm.; 13 9/16 × 9¾ in.

Provenance: Giorgio Vasari; (probably) Salomon Gautier; General John Guise.

Literature: Bell, p. 63; Colvin, I, 8, 9; Berenson, 1355A; A. Scharf, *Filippino Lippi*, 1935, Nos. 175, 188, 344, 345, 365; O. Kurz in *Old Master Drawings*, XII, 1937, Pls. 7, 8; K. B. Neilson, *Filippino Lippi*, 1938, pp. 142–144.

Exhibited: Royal Academy, 1930, No. 424; Matthiesen, 1960, No. 44; Liverpool, 1964, No. 27.

A is close in style to the British Museum drawing for the *Triumph of St. Thomas Aquinas* in S. Maria sopra Minerva, Rome (1488–

90). A drawing in the Uffizi (142E; exh. 1955, No. 38) is evidently for the same composition.

B may be somewhat later in date. The pricking suggests that it may have been used as a design for needlework. A small roundel of the same subject by Filippino is in the Pierpont Morgan Library.

C and D are probably only workshop-production; E is somewhat better and might be by the master. Scharf rejects all three.

The drawing attached to the *verso* is certainly not by Filippino, and no painter is known of the name of Altura Mantovano, to whom Vasari ascribed it. From the style one would guess it to be North Italian of about 1520–30. As C. F. Bell noted, the arms on the base of the frame are those of the Florentine family of Strozzi; but Dr. Middeldorf has observed that a branch of this family was equally prominent in Ferrara.

41 A MAN IN HEAVY DRAPERY, STANDING, HOLDING A STAFF IN HIS RIGHT HAND (0021)
Silverpoint, heightened with white, on slate blue ground.
209 × 127 mm.; 8¼ × 5 in.
Provenance: General John Guise.
Literature: Bell, A.16 (as School of Filippino); Berenson 853 (as Davide Ghirlandaio).

Surely by Filippino, in his Botticellesque manner, perhaps c. 1475, and of fine quality. Closely related to the studies on both sides of No. 39.

42 A LITTER-BEARER (0017)
Silverpoint, heightened with white, on pink ground.
180 × 132 mm.; 7 1/16 × 5 3/16 in.

Provenance: Padre Resta (the inscription below is in Resta's hand); John, Lord Somers (g.20); General John Guise.
Literature: Bell, A.12; Colvin, I, 14; Berenson 1354; Popham, *Italian Drawings at the R. A. 1930* (1931), p. 14; Scharf, *Filippino Lippi*, 1935, p. 125, No. 237.
Exhibited: Matthiesen, 1960, No. 45; Liverpool, 1964, No. 28.

This and a related drawing in the Uffizi, in which our figure is repeated with another added to the right (Scharf, Pl. 183), are apparently studies for the litter bearers in the *Raising of Drusiana*, one of Filippino's frescoes in the Strozzi chapel of S. Maria Novella in Florence. There is, however, no correspondence between either drawing and the figures in that fresco. The frescoes were finished in 1502, late in Filippino's career, and show throughout the extravagant mannerisms, in gesture, drapery, and ornament, that disfigure his late style. It is difficult to believe that the present beautiful drawing dates from that period; and in fact the commission to decorate the chapel was given to the artist by Filippo Strozzi as early as April 21, 1487 (Venturi, VII, part I, p. 644). Supposing, therefore, that the subjects to be depicted were agreed upon soon after that date, it seems likely that Filippino began immediately to make studies for individual figures.

I disagree strongly with the view expressed in Mr. Popham's catalogue of the Italian drawings at the Royal Academy in 1930 that the Christ Church drawing is a copy of the figure on the left of the Uffizi sheet, which was there exhibited as No. 437. The late Dr. Alfred Scharf (*op. cit.*) also disagreed with that view. The Christ Church study is rather more summary, and at the same time more spontaneous. It is in my opinion superior to, and earlier than, the other, which must have been made from it when Filippino was extending his ideas to include the second litter bearer and to relate them both to the litter.

Lombard School
Second quarter of XVI century

43 STUDY OF A YOUNG MAN WEARING A SWORD, RIGHT HAND RAISED (PERHAPS A COMMANDER ADDRESSING HIS TROOPS): fragment of a cartoon (1367)
Black chalk over red chalk, heightened with white body color, on four sheets of greenish grey paper, joined. Cut irregularly and laid down. Squared and pricked for transfer.
574×324 mm.; 18¹¹⁄₁₆×12¾ in. (max.)
Provenance: General John Guise.
Literature: Not in Bell.

An attribution to Giulio Campi, tentatively suggested both by Mr. Jacob Bean and Dr. Anna von Spitzmüller, is uncertain; but the drawing is by a very good hand, surely Lombard, of about 1530–40.

Studio of Andrea Mantegna
(Andrea Mantegna, c. 1430/31–1506)

44 HERCULES AND THE NEMEAN LION (0266)
Pen, brush, and brown wash on tawny yellow ground, elaborately heightened with white and yellow body color. Lower right corner torn away and roughly made up.
260×174 mm.; 10¼×6⅞ in.
Inscribed by the artist in white body color: D / HERC / IN / VICTO

Provenance: General John Guise.
Literature: Bell, H.12 (as School of Mantegna); Grosvenor Gallery Photographs, No. 12; Colvin, II, Pl. 28; A. M. Hind, *Corpus of Early Italian Engraving*, V, 1948, p. 36, No. 2; Popham and Pouncey, British Museum Cat., *Italian Drawings XIV–XV c.*, 1950, under No. 162.
Exhibited: Matthiesen, 1960, No. 46; Liverpool, 1964, No. 29.

This fine drawing, very close to Mantegna himself in style and technique, but not quite by his hand, seems to be the original used by Giovanni Antonio da Brescia for his signed engraving of the subject, which corresponds closely in the reverse direction (Hind, *op. cit.*, Pl. 526).

It is possible that the drawing is by Giovanni Antonio himself, copied from some drawing or grisaille-painting by Mantegna. We know nothing of his life, but he may have worked in Mantegna's studio towards the end of the XV century. Several of his plates derive from Mantegnesque designs, and these we may suppose to be the earlier ones; later he was influenced by Dürer, and later still by Marcantonio (see Hind, *op. cit.*, V, pp. 33–34).

A drawing of *Hercules and Antaeus* in the British Museum (cat. 1950, No. 162) seems to be almost certainly by the same hand, but as Popham and Pouncey emphasize, should not be regarded as a companion-piece. This too is related to an engraving of Mantegna's school (Hind 515), but so far as it corresponds it is in the same direction as the print.

The question of the authorship of these engravings of Mantegna's school, several of which exist in two or more versions engraved in opposite directions, and of certain drawings connected with them, is a very difficult one; I have discussed it to some extent in an article in *Old Master Drawings*, XI, March 1937.

Carlo Maratti
1625–1713

45 SELF-PORTRAIT (0621)
Black chalk with a little white on blue paper.
375 × 262 mm.; 14¾ × 10⅝ in.
Inscribed as a self-portrait of Maratta [sic] in the elder Richardson's hand on his mat below.
Provenance: J. Richardson sen. (L.2184); General John Guise.
Literature: Bell, s.8.

Described by Bell as "from the bust" on Maratti's monument in S. Maria degli Angeli, Rome. That bust is by Francesco Maratti, Carlo's son; but it is a mistake to suppose that the present drawing is copied from it; there is a general likeness, of course, but no exact correspondence. The sculpture in fact is much less sensitive; and I am convinced that the drawing is by Carlo Maratti's own hand, made with the aid of two mirrors, towards the end of his life. Earlier self-portrait drawings are in the Albertina and in the British Museum—the latter dated September 1684. The latest so far published is that at Düsseldorf, which is for the Stourhead painting of *c.* 1704–06. The Christ Church head can hardly be earlier than that; the artist's features are noticeably aged.

46 *Recto*: HEAD OF CHRIST, AND A KNEELING MAN
Verso: A NUDE WOMAN SEATED IN PROFILE TO LEFT, AND THE HEAD OF A WOMAN (VENUS?) SEEN FROM THE BACK (0730)
Red chalk.
413 × 275 mm.; 16 3/16 × 10 13/16 in.
Ascribed to Baccio Bandinelli in Richardson's hand on the old mat.
Provenance: Sir P. Lely (L.2092); W. Gibson (L.Suppl., p. 410); J. Richardson sen. (L.2184); General John Guise.
Literature: Bell, v.12 (as "anciently attributed to" Baccio Bandinelli).

The beautiful studies on the *recto* (perhaps for an *Agony in the Garden*) seem to me characteristic of Maratti at a fairly early date. The drawing must at least be earlier than 1680, since it belonged to Lely who died in that year.

The studies on the *verso* must be copies by Maratti from works of earlier masters—which misled Richardson into attributing the whole sheet to Bandinelli. The nude figure seated in profile seems likely to be copied from a painting or drawing by Bronzino or Alessandro Allori. The head seen from the back is surely from some antique statue, such as the Venere Urania now in the Uffizi; a similar figure appears in the background of Maratti's *Scuola del Disegno* (drawing at Chatsworth, No. 646; engraving by N. Dorigny); and a similar head in the right foreground of Maratti's drawing of *Apollo and Daphne* in the Albertina (cat. no. 798).

Michelangelo
1475–1564

47 *Recto*: A FAMILY GROUP: A WOMAN WITH A DISTAFF, THREE CHILDREN, A SLEEPING MAN AND A CAT
Verso: STUDIES OF A MAN'S LEG (0068)

Red chalk, with some black chalk on the *recto*.

212×283 mm.; 8⅜×11⅛ in.

Provenance: General John Guise.

Literature: Bell, B.21; J. C. Robinson, 1870, *A Critical Account. . .* , p. 103; Berenson 2493 and 1578[A]; Colvin, I, 37; Thode, *Kritische Untersuchungen*, 1908, p. 434; Steinmann, *Kunstchronik*, 1922/23, No. 835; Dussler, *Sebastiano del Piombo*, 1942, p. 173, No. 164; the same, *Michelangelos Zeichnungen*, 1959, p. 284, No. 636; J. Wilde, British Museum catalogue, *Michelangelo Drawings*, 1953, pp. 123–24.

Exhibited: British Museum, Michelangelo Exhibition, 1953, No. 35; Matthiesen, 1960, No. 49; Liverpool, 1964, No. 32.

The drawing on the *recto* is one of a group of chalk drawings formerly attributed (by Berenson, Dussler, and others) to Sebastiano del Piombo because they include studies for that artist's *Flagellation of Christ* in S. Pietro in Montorio, Rome (1516), and *Raising of Lazarus* now in the National Gallery, London (1519). Johannes Wilde, however, maintained the attribution of the drawings to Michelangelo, pointing to Vasari's statement that Michelangelo supplied drawings to help his friend Sebastiano, particularly in the case of the *Lazarus*. This view, which is now widely accepted, seems to be supported by the contrast in style between the *recto* of the Christ Church sheet and the drawing of rather similar content at Windsor Castle, (Popham and Wilde No. 923, Pl. 80), which is certainly by Sebastiano.

Robinson observed that the composition of the *recto* (which can hardly be intended for a *Holy Family*) recalls the groups of the Ancestors of Christ in the Sistine ceiling.

The beautiful leg-study on the *verso* has been generally accepted as Michelangelo's, even by those (including Berenson) who attributed the *recto* to Sebastiano. Only Dussler rejected it (1959, *loc. cit.*), for reasons which I do not appreciate. The drawing is in fact of the highest quality. A close copy is in the British Museum (Wilde, No. 86 and Pl. CXXXIX).

Wilde and Popham date the drawing 1515–20.

48   THE GOOD THIEF (?) ON THE CROSS, WITH INSCRIPTIONS IN MICHELANGELO'S HAND (0094)

On the *verso*, rough anatomical (?) sketches in black chalk and the name *Andrea* in Michelangelo's hand.

Black chalk with some pen and brown ink.

162×101 mm.; 6⅜×4 in.

The two lines in Michelangelo's hand at the top read: *un ultra sera p[erch]e stasera piove / e mal puo dir chi e spectato altrove.* Sideways on the sheet is another inscription (eight lines of verse?) also in the artist's hand but scribbled out (the words *dove duola* still legible); and at the side of this, below, a contemporary inscription in another hand.

Provenance: General John Guise.

Literature: Bell, C.13; J. C. Robinson, *Critical Account*, 1870, p. 103, No. 2; Berenson 1578; Frey, II, 1909–11, No. 139a and b; Thode, 1913, No. 456; Goldscheider, 1951, No. 37; Wilde, British Museum catalogue, 1953, p. 62, No. 30; Dussler, 1959, p. 191, No. 353; Tolnay in Quaderno N.153 of the Accademia Nazionale dei Lincei, 1971,

Alcune recenti scoperte e risultati negli studi Michelangioleschi, p. 19 and Pl. xxxiiA. Exhibited: British Museum, Michelangelo Exhibition, 1953, No. 110; Matthiesen, 1960, No. 48; Liverpool, 1964, No. 31.

Berenson and Goldscheider both date the drawing c. 1515, but all other writers suggest a later date: Dussler c. 1530, Frey late 1530s. The handwriting seems to support the later date, and in a recent article (1971, *loc. cit.*) Tolnay connects the Christ Church drawing and one in Count Seilern's collection with a small wooden *bozzetto* in the Casa Buonarotti (*ibid.*, Pl. xxxiii), which he dates to the end of Michelangelo's career.

The figure has generally been described as Christ on the Cross, but the upward turn of the head might suggest that it was in fact intended for the Good Thief in a Crucifixion.

Pier Francesco Mola
1612–1666

49   TWO CHILDREN PLAYING WITH RABBITS IN A CAGE; AND ANOTHER PLAYING WITH A KITTEN   (0576)
Pen and brown wash over black chalk, with a little pink watercolor. Torn and made up on left and below.
120 × 170 mm.; 4¾ × 6¹¹⁄₁₆ in. (irregular)
Inscribed in the artist's hand, to explain the subject: (*two children playing with a cage with Rabbits inside it* and *child holding a Kitten and squeezing it . . . and the Kitten is about to scratch him with its paw*).
Provenance: General John Guise.
Literature: Bell, Q.34.

A particularly charming example of Mola's genre.

Lelio Orsi
1511(?)–1587

50   THE VIRGIN AND CHILD SEATED IN THE WINDOW EMBRASURE OF A COLONNADE: SS. ANDREW AND JUDE BELOW   (1349)
Pen, brush, and brown wash on buff-grounded paper heightened with white body color. Partly squared in black chalk.
367 × 216 mm.; 14⁷⁄₁₆ × 8½ in.
Provenance: General John Guise.
Literature: Not in Bell.

An important and entirely characteristic example of Orsi's rather bizarre style. The figures, particularly the Virgin and Child, make the effect of having been drawn from sculpture; but this group is in fact very Correggesque, and must surely have been inspired by some such painting as the *Madonna of the Basket*, No. 23 of the National Gallery.

Parmigianino (Francesco Mazzola)
1503–1540

51   DESIGNS FOR THREE ORNAMENTAL PANELS:
(a) with a female figure below, and a kneeling angel above (0412); (b) with St. John the Evangelist (0413); (c) with a bearded male figure (0414)
Pen and brown wash with watercolor and body color.
Respectively, 111 × 29 mm.; 4³⁄₈ × 1⅛ in., 102 × 42 mm.; 4 × 1⅝ in., 97 × 29 mm.; 3¹³⁄₁₆ × 1⅛ in.
Provenance: Lanière (L.2886); Sir P. Lely (L.2092); General John Guise.

Literature: Bell, M.19^{A, B, C}; A. E. Popham, *Catalogue of the Drawings of Parmigianino*, 1971, I, pp. 22–25 and 131, Nos. 347–349, Pl. 325.

Perhaps originally all parts of the same sheet, these slight but charming sketches were identified by Popham as for the decoration of one of the *sottarchi*—i.e., the soffits of the arches dividing the vaulting from the apse on one side and the central cupola on the other—in the church of S. Maria della Steccata at Parma. This was only a small part of the work mentioned in a document of May 10, 1531, which Parmigianino agreed to finish by November of the following year. It was his delay and neglect in fulfilling this contract that led to his arrest and imprisonment in summer 1539, and to his departure in disgrace for Casalmaggiore, where he died a year later.

Bartolommeo Passarotti
1529–1592

52 STUDIES FOR THE ADORATION OF THE KINGS (1393)
Pen and brown ink and grey wash, over black chalk (only on the figure extreme right). A strip along the top, approximately 22 mm. deep (including the turban of the third king), is an early restoration.
430 × 562 mm.; 16⅞/₁₆ × 18⅜/₁₆ in.
Provenance: General John Guise.
Literature: Not in Bell.

This important drawing is clearly a preparatory study for the altarpiece of the *Adoration of the Kings* in the Archiepiscopal Palace at Bologna (repr. *Belvedere*, 1938–39, XIII, 1/4, Fig. 84). The draped figures in the drawing correspond to those of the three kings in the painting, with some variations. The nude studies to left and right, which relate to the figures of the two standing kings, must have been drawn subsequently to the draped figures.

The draped study in the center (the figure seen from the back) seems to have been used with some modifications by Tiburzio Passarotti, Bartolommeo's son, for the apostle on the right of his *Assumption of the Virgin* in the church of S. Maria della Purificazione at Bologna.

Pietro Perugino
1450–1523

53 BUST OF A BEARDED MAN: fragment of a cartoon   (0122)
Black chalk. Pricked for transfer, and squared. A second piece of paper (original) joined below. Irregularly cut and roughly made up above.
270 × 250 mm.; 10⅝ × 9⅞ in. (max.)
Provenance: General John Guise.
Literature: Bell, D.12; O. Fischel in *Jahrbuch der Preussischen Kunstsammlungen*, XXXVIII, 1917, p. 107, No. 42 and Fig. 112.
Exhibited: Royal Academy, 1953, No. 37; Matthiesen, 1960, No. 56; Liverpool, 1964, No. 35.

First identified by J. C. Robinson in 1868 as part of the cartoon for the figure of Joseph of Arimathaea kneeling on the left, supporting the body of Christ, in Perugino's *Deposition* in the Pitti Gallery, Florence. The drawing is of great importance as an example of a cartoon bearing all the marks of use in the production of the painting concerned, yet retaining all its quality. Fischel (*loc. cit.*)

draws attention to a brush drawing of the same head in the Louvre (No. 4383), which he considers a good copy from the painting.

Baldassarre Peruzzi
1481–1536

54 AN ALLEGORY OF
   FORTUNE (0137)
Pen and brown ink over black chalk. Mostly pricked for transfer.
273 × 204 mm.; 10³⁄₄ × 8 in.
Provenance: Sir P. Lely (L.2092); William Gibson (L.Suppl. 2885); General John Guise.
Literature: Bell, D.27; D. von Hadeln in *Burlington Magazine*, XLVIII, 1926, p. 301; C. L. Frommel, *Baldassarre Peruzzi als Maler und Zeichner*, Bibliotheca Hertziana, 1967–68, No. 100 and Pl. LXXVᵃ.
Exhibited: Matthiesen, 1960, No. 58; Liverpool, 1964, No. 36.

Baron von Hadeln observed that this fine drawing was reproduced in reverse in the woodcut title page to Sigismondo Fanti's *Triompho di Fortuna*, printed in Venice in January 1527 by Agostino da Portese for Giacomo Giunta; but Hadeln discarded the old attribution to Peruzzi (on the backing, in a late-XVII-century hand) for one to Dosso Dossi, which is certainly wrong. Peruzzi is not known to have had any connection with Venice, and the drawing may have been pirated by the Venetian publisher. The other cuts in the book were not designed by him.

It is interesting to note that though most of the contours are pricked, those of the nude figure on the right, holding a box, are not; and this figure is in fact considerably altered in the woodcut.

Studio of Pisanello
(Antonio Pisano, c. 1395–c. 1455)

55 *Recto*: HEAD OF A PILGRIM
   Verso: A NAKED CHILD
   HOLDING A STAFF (0255)
Pen and pale brown wash on paper partly grounded pink. *Verso* in red chalk, worked over in pen and ink, also on pink ground.
250 × 165 mm.; 9⁷⁄₈ × 6¹⁄₂ in.
Provenance: Ridolfi; General John Guise.
Literature: Bell, H.1; G. F. Hill in *Vasari Society*, 1st series, 1912–1913, Pl. 1; M. Fossi-Todorow, *I Disegni del Pisanello e della sua Cerchia*, 1966, p. 104, No. 106.

Hill considered the pilgrim's head to be a study, by an assistant of Pisanello (perhaps Bono da Ferrara), for the figure in the fresco of the Pellegrini shield in the chapel of that name in S. Anastasia, Verona. The head in that fresco is very similar, but there is no exact correspondence. The drawing is surely contemporary and the pilgrim on the *recto* has a certain rough grandeur, but it is certainly inferior to the best of the famous Vallardi album in the Louvre; and the child on the *verso* is very crudely drawn. It may be a studio copy from a lost original study by Pisanello. Dottoressa M. Fossi-Todorow (*loc. cit.*) shares this view.

Polidoro da Caravaggio
1490/1500–1543?

56 STUDIES FOR ST. JEROME
   IN PENITENCE (0392)
Red chalk.
148 × 142 mm.; 5¹³⁄₁₆ × 5⁹⁄₁₆ in.

Provenance: Sir Peter Lely (L.2092); William Gibson (d. 1703) (his price-mark on back; for a note on Gibson, who bought extensively at the Lely sale in 1688, see Lugt, Supplément, under No. 2885); General John Guise.
Literature: Bell, M.6 (as by Correggio).
Exhibited: Royal Academy, 1960, No. 584.

A good and very characteristic sheet of studies by Polidoro, comparable in style and type to the *Bearded Man wearing a Cloak*, also from the Lely Collection, in the British Museum (Pouncey and Gere, 1962, No. 207).

Cesare Pollini
c. 1560–*c.* 1630

57   THE HOLY FAMILY, AND TWO SEPARATE STUDIES OF A PAIR OF NAKED CHILDREN (0742)
On the *verso*, visible through the backing, are various other sketches: a pair of male profiles, two putti, etc.
Pen and brown wash over red chalk.
198 × 265 mm.; 7$\frac{13}{16}$ × 10$\frac{7}{16}$ in.
Provenance: General John Guise.
Literature: Bell, w.5 (as Italian, 1575–1625).

Starting from this attractive drawing, which is inscribed in a XVII-century hand, Mr. P. M. R. Pouncey has identified a number of others by Pollini, several of similar subject to ours, and in the same characteristic technique.

The artist is recorded as a miniaturist, from Perugia, and two miniatures by him of groups of putti dancing (one group clothed, the other naked) under the sacred mono-

gram are in the Manuscripts Department of the British Museum.

Jacopo Pontormo
1494–1557

58   THE DEPOSITION (1336)
Black chalk, lightly washed over, heightened with body color. Squared in red chalk. The outlines of the upper figures reinforced, apparently with a stilus.
443 × 276 mm.; 17$\frac{7}{16}$ × 10$\frac{7}{8}$ in. Arched top.
Provenance: Jonathan Richardson sen. (L.2184); General John Guise.
Literature: Not in Bell; W. R. Jeudwine in *Apollo*, April 1959, p. 114; Berenson, 1961 ed., I, p. 461 (footnote); P. M. R. Pouncey in *Master Drawings*, II, 1964, p. 290; Janet Cox-Rearick, *The Drawings of Pontormo*, 1964, No. 272 and Pl. 254; Catherine Monbeig-Goguel, *Il Manierismo Fiorentino*, 1971, p. 81 and Pl. IV.
Exhibited: Matthiesen, 1960, No. 60; Liverpool, 1964, No. 37; Manchester, 1965, No. 360.

This very important drawing, overlooked at Christ Church until comparatively recent times, is the composition-study for Pontormo's masterpiece in the Capponi Chapel of S. Felicità, Florence, painted *c.* 1526–28, for which various detail studies exist in the Uffizi and the British Museum (Cox-Rearick, Nos. 267–277).

There are considerable variations in the painting. Most remarkable perhaps, as Janet Cox-Rearick observes, is the way in which the weight of the composition has been shifted upwards: the feet and legs of the three lower figures in the painting are smaller and slighter, and much less functionally posed; the youth supporting the legs of Christ is no longer kneeling, but squatting on one heel. The whole effect of the altarpiece is less realistic, more in the Mannerist taste.

Except in the top quarter, where the outlines have been reworked with the stilus and perhaps with the pen, the drawing is of superb quality and outstanding beauty.

Raffaellino del Garbo
1466–1524

59   THE VIRGIN AND CHILD WITH S. CATHERINE AND THE MAGDALEN; a roundel (0051)
Pen and brown ink on pinkish-brown toned paper, heightened with white.
278 mm.; 10⅟₁₆ in. in diameter.
Provenance: General John Guise.
Literature: Bell, B.5; Grosvenor Gallery Photographs, No. 44; Colvin, I, 11; Berenson 768; Van Marle, XII, 1930, pp. 416ff.; A. Scharf, *Jahrbuch der Preussischen Kunstsammlungen*, 1933, p. 163. J. Byam Shaw, *Catalogue of Paintings by Old Masters at Christ Church, Oxford*, 1967, under No. 48.
Exhibited: Matthiesen, 1960, No. 22.

In spite of damage, the drawing is a fine and characteristic example of Raffaellino at his best. It has been supposed to be a preliminary for the National Gallery *tondo* (Berenson, *Florentine School*, 1963, Pl. 1165, and *Florentine Drawings*, 3rd ed., 1961, Fig. 249), but there is no correspondence except in the subject, and our drawing is perhaps more related in style to the *tondo* at Christ Church (Byam Shaw, *loc. cit.*). It is much less Filippinesque than the studies of the Madonna in

the British Museum (Popham and Pouncey, 1950, No. 63), attributed to Raffaellino but very close to Filippino himself; if these are really by Raffaellino they must be earlier than ours, perhaps of the late 1480s. Ours might then be of the second half of the next decade.

Raphael
1483–1520

60   SEVEN PUTTI PLAYING (0112)
Pen and brown ink.
145 × 214 mm.; 5⅟₁₆ × 8⅞ in.
Provenance: Lanière (small star, L.2886); Richardson sen.ʳ (L.2184); General John Guise.
Literature: Bell, D.2; Passavant, *Tour*, 1836, II, p. 131; the same, *Raphael*, 1860, p. 551; J. C. Robinson, *Critical Account*, 1870, p. 315, No. 2; Ruland, *The works of Raphael . . .*, 1876, p. 141, VIII, No. 1; Crowe and Cavalcaselle, *Raphael*, 1885, II, p. 547; O. Fischel, *Raphaels Zeichnungen, Versuch einer Kritik*, 1898, p. 186, No. 491; the same, *Raphaels Zeichnungen*, II, 1919, p. 125, No. 102; K. T. Parker, Ashmolean catalogue, II, 1956, p. 275.
Exhibited: Matthiesen, 1960, No. 61; Liverpool, 1964, No. 38.

Reproduced in the reverse direction in Pond and Knapton's series of facsimile etchings, when still in the collection of Jonathan Richardson senior.

The drawing must date from about 1507–08. The children appear to be playing at "Judge and Prisoner," the "Judge" enthroned on a large urn. A similar subject occurs on the *verso* of a drawing in the Ashmolean Museum, Oxford (Parker, cat. no. 528), which Parker supposes to have been reworked. Fischel suggests that it may have been inspired by the friezes of playing putti on Donatello's pulpits in S. Lorenzo, Florence; a small bronze ascribed to Donatello in Berlin (Phaidon Press, *Donatello*, 1941, p. 42, Fig. 136) is also comparable.

Guido Reni
1575–1642

61 STUDY FOR THE HEAD OF
ST. PROCULUS (0528)
Black chalk, with a little red and white.
338 × 260 mm.; 13 5/16 × 10 1/4 in.
Provenance: Padre Resta; John, Lord Somers (e.80, wrongly transcribed *c.80*); General John Guise.
Literature: Bell, P.24; Guido Reni Exhibition, Bologna, 1954, under No. 35.
Exhibited: Royal Academy, No. 397 (wrongly described as for the head of St. Proculus in the *Pietà with five Saints* at Bologna).

This fine drawing is for the head of St. Proculus, one of the patron saints of Bologna, standing on the extreme right of one of Guido's most famous works, the *Palio della Peste* now in the Pinacoteca of that city, which was painted for the Palazzo Pubblico as a thank-offering to the Virgin for deliverance from the plague of 1630–31. Originally a banner (*Paglione del Voto* or *Palio della Peste*), it was carried annually in procession to the church of S. Domenico. The study corresponds fairly closely to the head in the painting, except for the hair and the neck.

Roman (?) School
Early XVII century

62 DESIGN FOR THE FRIEZE
OF A ROOM (0958)
Pen and watercolor over black chalk.
215 × 387 mm.; 8 1/2 × 15 1/4 in.
With many inscriptions by the artist.
Provenance: General John Guise.
Literature: Bell, CC.27 (as by Niccolò Berrettoni).

In the inscription at the top, so far as I can decipher it, the artist seems to offer to his patron this design for the decoration of an entrance-hall; and adds that there are other designs available. The other inscriptions refer to the individual features of the decoration, part of which was no doubt intended to be executed in stucco. They are written in a very illiterate style.

This attractive and interesting drawing is surely of an earlier date than Maratti's pupil, Niccolò Berrettoni, to whom it was once attributed. Rather similar schemes of decoration by Giovanni and Cherubino Alberti in the Palazzo Ruggieri, Rome, and also in the Sala Clementina of the Vatican, are illustrated by Maria Brugnoli in *Bollettino d'Arte*, XLV, 1960, pp. 223ff.

Giovanni Battista Rosso, called Rosso Fiorentino
1494–1540

63 ST. JOHN THE BAPTIST
PREACHING (?) (1148)
Red chalk, rubbed over. All corners cut. The hand of the man holding a staff, at the extreme left, is retouched with the pen. Indented with the stilus.

263 × 152 mm.; 10⅜ × 6 in.
Provenance: General John Guise.
Literature: Not in Bell.

The truncated right arm of the figure seated in the foreground left seems to be a caprice of the artist, suggested no doubt by the famous *Torso di Belvedere* in the Vatican, which was clearly the source of inspiration here. The same curious feature occurs in a drawing of a *Group of nude Figures* in the Uffizi (Venturi, IX, 5, Fig. 125). The strange types have much in common with some of those in Rosso's famous altarpiece of the *Deposition* at Volterra, dated 1521, and the date of our drawing cannot be much later.

64 AN ORNAMENTAL PANEL, WITH SCENES ILLUSTRATING PETRARCH (*Rime*, No. CCCXXIII) (1337)
Pen and brown ink, with grey wash, heightened with white body color on brown prepared paper.
425 × 536 mm.; 16¾ × 17³⁄₁₆ in.
Provenance: Sir P. Lely (L.2092); General John Guise.
Literature: Bell, p. 83 (large portfolio) (as by Salimbeni).
Exhibited: Manchester, 1965, *European Art 1520–1600*, No. 371.

The arms may be almost certainly identified as those of the Cardinal Jean de Lorraine (1498–1550), who received the hat in 1518. His arms as illustrated in Ciaconius, 1677, III, p. 418, show two more quarterings, 6 (for Guelderland—a lion crowned, or) and 7 (for Julich—a lion sable); but the Cardinal may have added these only on the death of his mother, Philippa of Guelderland, in 1547, when Rosso was already dead. Two nephews of Cardinal Jean, Charles and Louis de Guise, became cardinals in 1534 and 1550 respectively; but their arms both show the extra quarterings and other differences.

The drawing, which is of excellent quality and surely original, must therefore date within the last ten years of Rosso's life, spent entirely in France, in Paris or at Fontainebleau. It illustrates very literally the text of Petrarch that is carefully inscribed by the artist on the tablet in the center ("As I stood one day alone at the window, from which I saw so many new things that I was almost tired, just of watching, a wild beast appeared on my right hand, with a human face of such beauty as to enamour Jove himself; hunted by two hounds, one black, one white . . ."). The whole suggests a tapestry; but Mr. Eugene Carroll has pointed out to me that the lengthy inscription from Petrarch's *Rime* would be ill suited to weaving, and it is perhaps more likely that the design was intended to be carried out in painting and stucco on a wall, like Rosso's decorations in the Gallery of Francis I at Fontainebleau, for which payments are recorded between 1536 and 1540. For the border, we may compare that of the engraving of the *Nymph of Fontainebleau* by Réné Boyvin after Rosso (repr. Kusenberg, *Il Rosso*, 1931, Pl. LXI).

It is possible that General Guise's interest in this drawing may be partly explained by a wish to associate himself with the very distinguished French family of Guise, to which the Cardinal belonged.

The handwriting of the inscription accords very well with the specimen of Rosso's hand reproduced by Kusenberg, *op. cit.*, Pl. XXX.

Francesco Salviati
1510–1563

65 DESIGN FOR A SACRED
VESSEL, PROBABLY A
CIBORIUM OR CHALICE
(1371)
Pen and brown wash over black chalk,
delicately hatched with white body
color, on buff paper. Top corners cut.
632×244 mm.; 24⅞×9⅝ in. (including an added strip of 61 mm. [2⅜ in.]
at the bottom).
Provenance: General John Guise.
Literature: Not in Bell; Catherine
Monbeig-Goguel, *Il Manierismo Fiorentino*, pp. 90–91 and Fig. 23.

A fine example of Salviati's work as a designer of silver- and goldsmith's ware. A design for a ewer, secular in purpose, in the
Ashmolean Museum (Parker, II, No. 683,
Pl. CLII) is comparable in style.

The figure of the risen Christ at the top,
remotely reminiscent of Michelangelo's
marble in S. Maria sopra Minerva in Rome,
makes it certain that the vessel was intended
for a religious purpose, but what that purpose was is not clear. Father Anthony Levi
thinks that this is certainly not a monstrance,
but probably a ciborium, to hold the com-
munion wafers, or a chalice for the wine; in
which case the top part, with the figure of
Christ and the cherubs round his feet, would
be the cover. Father Levi's suggestion is supported by comparison with a ciborium from
Chapelle du Saint-Esprit, c. 1530–35, now in
the Louvre, which is to some extent similar
in design (repd. *Apollo*, XC, October 1969,
p. 294).

The winged genii supporting a wreath
round the stem may be Virtues, triumphing
over the Vices or pagan Deities crushed under the base.

The strip at the bottom, including the figures round the side of the base, is more freely
drawn than the rest, but is certainly an addition by the artist himself.

66 DESIGN FOR A CLOCK,
WITH THE MEDICI ARMS,
SUPPORTING FIGURES OF
FAITH AND HOPE, AND
FIGURES REPRESENTING
THE FOUR SEASONS
ROUND THE CLOCK FACE
(0985)
Black chalk and bistre wash.
418×271 mm.; 16⁷⁄₁₆×10¹¹⁄₁₆ in.
Provenance: General John Guise.
Literature: Bell, DD.18 (as "anciently
attributed to Andrea del Sarto"); Cath-
erine Monbeig-Goguel in *Revue de
l'Art*, No. 14, 1971, p. 110 and Fig. 6.

The present attribution was first made by
Mr. Philip Pouncey; Mme Monbeig-Goguel's attribution to Jacopo Zucchi is less
convincing. Seven ornament drawings in the
Uffizi, in red chalk and brown wash (Nos.
936–940.0, 9420.0, and 9430.0), are comparable, but are all inferior to ours, and I believe
only studio copies. Of these, Uffizi 943 is in
fact a (much inferior) replica of Uffizi 942.

Sebastiano del Piombo
1485–1547

67 STUDY FOR THE HEAD OF
THE VIRGIN MARY (1160)
Black chalk, slightly heightened with
white body color, on blue paper dis-
colored green.
92×84 mm.; 3⅝×3⁵⁄₁₆ in.

Provenance: Padre Resta; John, Lord Somers (*c.12*); General John Guise.
Literature: Not in Bell; J. Byam Shaw in *Master Drawings*, VI, 1968, p. 242 and Pl. I.

The study seems certainly to have been used for Sebastiano's *Madonna del Velo* now in Naples, but its date may be rather later than I suggested in my note of 1968. As Mr. Michael Hirst has observed, traces of the Venetian influences to which I drew attention remain constant in Sebastiano's work, and this (and the painting) may be as late as the mid-1530s. A drawing in the Louvre (M. Hirst in *Burlington Magazine*, CVII, 1965, p. 177, Fig. 5) may be from the same model wearing the same cap; and that is certainly a study for the Duke of Northumberland's *Visitation*—a very late work.

Elisabetta Sirani
1638–1664

68 SELF-PORTRAIT (0575)
Black, red, and a little white chalk, on blue-grey paper.
386×270 mm.; 15 3/16 × 10 5/8 in.
Provenance: General John Guise.
Literature: Bell, Q.33.

A small round painting on panel, exhibited at the Heim Gallery, London, in Autumn 1968 (cat. no. 21), as a self-portrait of Elisabetta Sirani, seems to be of the same model, though the arrangement of the hair is different. A drawing of a whole-length figure in the Ashmolean Museum is inscribed as her self-portrait in an XVIII-century hand; and Sir Karl Parker in his catalogue entry (II, No. 953) refers to another painting in the W. Roscoe sale at Liverpool, September 25, 1816 (No. 413).

Elisabetta Sirani died at the age of twenty-six; the date of this drawing may therefore be about 1660.

Giovanni Antonio Bazzi, called Sodoma
1477–1549

69 BUST PORTRAIT OF A YOUNG MAN, SUPPOSED TO BE RAPHAEL (0070)
Black chalk with body color, washed over.
404×288 mm.; 15 15/16 × 11 5/16 in.
Provenance: Vasari (?) (the ascription to Leonardo, and what remains of the old border, seem to be his); Benedetto Luti (?); William Kent (?); General John Guise.
Literature: Bell, B.23; Passavant, *Tour* (English ed., 1836), p. 133; Robinson, *Critical Account*, 1870, p. 319; No. 10; G. Frizzoni in *L'Arte*, VII, 1904, p. 98; C. Ricci in *Rassegna d'Arte*, V, 1905, p. 775; H. Cust, *Giov. Ant. Bazzi*, 1906, p. 114; Colvin, 1907, I, 26; P. Schubring, *Die Kunst der Hochrenaissance in Italien*, 1926, Pl. XXV; Popham, *Italian Drawings*, 1931, No. 243; Hugo Wagner, *Raffael im Bildnis*, 1969, pp. 45–47; Anna Forlani Tempesti, *Capolavori del rinascimento (Disegni dei Maestri)*, 1970, p. 86.
Exhibited: Royal Academy, 1930, No. 637; Royal Academy, 1953, No. 45; Matthiesen, 1960, No. 70; Liverpool, 1964, No. 45.

The attribution of this rather celebrated drawing to Sodoma was first proposed by Frizzoni (*loc. cit*), and is now generally accepted. It is close in style, especially in the parts that are more freely drawn, to the fine cartoon of the *Holy Family* in the Ashmolean Museum, Oxford (Parker cat., II, No. 700 and Pl. CLVI).

The identification as a portrait of Raphael had been generally rejected in the more recent literature, until Dr. Wagner revived the discussion in his book on that subject in 1969, and expressed a more favorable view. He supposes that the portrait was drawn by Sodoma in Siena *c.* 1504, when Raphael was twenty-one—though there is no certain evidence that Raphael was in Siena in that year. He compares the head of a boy in the British Museum, which Pouncey and Gere are strongly inclined to accept as a self-portrait of Raphael, *c.* 1500 (British Museum catalogue, 1962, p. 2, No. 1 *verso*, and Pl. 1). The resemblance is not entirely convincing. The lips in the Christ Church drawing are very full, and the mouth is not like that of the accepted self-portrait on the right of the *School of Athens*; but some grey wash has been used to define the form of the upper lip, and I am not sure that this is original. There seems to be some restoration in the face generally.

Antonio Tempesta
1555–1630

70 A LION HUNT (1395)
Pen and bistre and blue-grey wash over rough black chalk.
362 × 655 mm.; 14¼ × 25¹³⁄₁₆ in.
Provenance: General John Guise.
Literature: Bell, p. 86 (large portfolio).

An excellent and characteristic drawing by this Florentine master, who was famous for his battle- and hunting-scenes, as a painter, etcher, and designer for tapestry. He worked extensively in the Vatican.

Domenico Tintoretto
1560–1635

71 THE MARTYRDOM OF ST. STEPHEN: sketch for an altarpiece (0365)
Oils (monochrome) on blue paper. Squared for enlargement, apparently with the butt of the brush in the wet paint.
345 × 187 mm.; 13⁹⁄₁₆ × 7⅜ in.
Provenance: J. Richardson sen. (?); General John Guise.
Literature: Bell, L.12 (as by Jacopo Tintoretto); D. von Hadeln, *Zeichnungen des Giacomo Tintoretto*, 1922, Pl. 72; Venturi, IX, 4 (1929), p. 656; Tozzi in *Bollettino d'Arte*, XL, 1937, p. 24, Fig. 5; H. and E. Tietze, 1944, No. 1536 (all except Bell as Domenico T.).
Exhibited: Venice, Fondazione Giorgio Cini, 1958, *Disegni Veneti di Oxford*, No. 54.

The sketch corresponds fairly closely, in its main features, to the altarpiece in S. Giorgio Maggiore, Venice (Tietze, *Tintoretto*, 1948, Fig. 278), the commission for which was given to Jacopo Tintoretto in 1593, the year before his death, when he was already at work on the two vast canvases of the *Gathering of the Manna* and the *Last Supper* for the choir of the same church. This lends probability to the contention of Venturi, Hadeln, and others that the altarpiece of the *Martyrdom of St. Stephen* must be largely the work of Domenico, painted no doubt under his father's supervision. In any case the Christ Church drawing is exactly in the style of a group of oil sketches in the British Museum that is now generally agreed to be by Domenico's hand. These brilliant sketches, as the Tietzes remark, greatly enhance the stature of Domenico as an independent artist, and certainly bear comparison with his father's work.

Jacopo Tintoretto
1518–1594

72 HEAD OF GIULIANO DE' MEDICI, AFTER MICHELANGELO (0357)
Charcoal, with a little white chalk, on faded blue paper.
357×238 mm.; 14$\frac{1}{16}$×9$\frac{3}{8}$ in.
Provenance: General John Guise.
Literature: Bell, L.4; Colvin, II, 42; D. von Hadeln, *Zeichnungen des Giacomo Tintoretto*, 1922, p. 27, Pl. 9; Popham, *Italian Drawings*, 1931, No. 279; A. Morassi, Cat. of the Rasini Collection, Milan, 1937, in note to Pl. XXIX; H. and E. Tietze, *Drawings of the Venetian Painters*, 1944, No. 1731.
Exhibited: Royal Academy, 1930, No. 677; Venice, 1958, Fondazione Giorgio Cini, *Disegni Veneti di Oxford*, No. 50; Matthiesen, 1960, No. 73; Liverpool, 1964, No. 46.

This beautiful drawing must have been made either from a cast of the head of Michelangelo's statue in the Medici chapel of S. Lorenzo in Florence, or from the head of a small *modello* for the whole figure that was used by Tintoretto for other drawings (two of them also at Christ Church, inv. nos. 0354 and 0355). The view in the present drawing corresponds nearly to that of the detail of the original head reproduced by Tolnay, *Michelangelo*, III, 1948, Pl. 45. On Tintoretto's use of casts, and also of small copies of Michelangelo's sculptures made by Daniele da Vol-

terra, see Ridolfi, *Meraviglie . . .*, 1648, Pt. II p. 6.

In the Rasini Collection at Milan is a version of this head probably by Marietta Tintoretto, the artist's elder daughter; it is drawn on the *verso* of a *Head of Vitellius* (Morassi, *loc. cit.*, Pl. XXVIII), which bears a contemporary ascription to Marietta. I disagree emphatically with Morassi's suggestion that the Christ Church drawing is also by her, and that the version in the Uffizi (inv. no. 1841, Gernsheim photo. 10307) is better. The Uffizi version seems to me inferior, though possibly also by Jacopo himself.

Titian (Tiziano Vecelli)
c. 1480–1576

73 THE VIRGIN AND CHILD ENTHRONED ON A HIGH PEDESTAL; a child angel playing a viol on the step below; on the right, a winged cherub's head in profile to left (0284)
Red chalk, partly drawn over with pen and brown ink. The cherub's head right entirely in pen and ink.
265×185 mm.; 10$\frac{7}{16}$×7$\frac{5}{16}$ in.
Provenance: Sir P. Lely (L.2092); General John Guise.
Literature: Bell, H.28 (as Venetian School, *c.* 1500); G. Frizzoni in *L'Arte*, XI, 1908, p. 174 (as Titian); R. von Beckerath in *Repertorium für Kunstwissenschaft*, XXXI, 1908, p. 112 (as Pordenone); Colvin, II, 39 (as Venetian, *c.* 1520); D. von Hadeln in *Jahrbuch der Preussischen Kunstsammlungen*, XXXIV, 1913, p. 244 (as Francesco Vecelli); R. Longhi in *L'Arte*, XX, 1917, p. 359 (as Titian) (reprinted with *Scritti Giovanili* in Longhi's col-

lected works, 1961, I, p. 389); D. von Hadeln, *Zeichnungen des Tizian*, 1924, Pl. 40; H. and E. Tietze, *Drawings of the Venetian Painters*, 1944, p. 333, No. 2019; G. Fiocco in *The Connoisseur*, November 1955, p. 166 and Fig. 3 (as Francesco Vecelli); K. T. Parker, catalogue of Fondazione Giorgio Cini exhibition, 1958, No. 21.

Exhibited: Venice, 1958, Fondazione Giorgio Cini, *Disegni Veneti di Oxford*, No. 21.

Baron von Hadeln (1913) was the first to observe that this drawing (of which he gives a grossly distorted reproduction) corresponds to a considerable extent with a small altarpiece, now in Berlin, which was attributed by a near-contemporary authority to Francesco Vecelli—supposedly (but not certainly) the elder brother of Titian, a mediocre artist on his own account who gave up painting to join the Venetian army. The Berlin picture (see Fiocco, *loc. cit.*, for a reproduction after cleaning) seems to be of a debased Bellinesque-Giorgionesque type; and to my mind the Christ Church drawing is greatly superior to it precisely in those respects in which the correspondence exists. The two works are simply not on the same artistic level.

The drawing has suffered in reputation from very poor reproductions, and the original has not often been exhibited. I believe it to be most probably by the great master's hand, at an early date, c. 1510–15, much in the style (as Frizzoni said many years ago) of the "Gipsy" Madonna in Vienna. I do not agree with Sir Karl Parker (*loc. cit.*) in thinking the penwork by a later hand.

The question remains, whether this drawing was used by Francesco for the painting now in Berlin (from the church of S. Croce, Belluno), or whether it was done by Titian as a record, perhaps a subconscious criticism, of his brother's performance. Longhi, who repudiated Hadeln's attribution, supposed that it was a study for a lost altarpiece by Titian himself, which was copied (in the Berlin painting) by his brother; but against that it must be said that the Berlin painting is much less "Titianesque" in character than the Christ Church drawing.

There is in the Berlin Printroom a drawing for the second angel musician, who plays a tambourine, in the Berlin painting (Tietzes, 1944, No. 2017 and Pl. LXXXII). It is in a metal-point and brush technique entirely different from that of the present drawing. It could hardly be by the same hand, but might indeed be by Francesco Vecelli himself.

Niccolò Martinelli da Pesaro, called Trometta
c. 1540/45–after 1605

74 DESIGN FOR PART OF THE DECORATION OF A FAÇADE, WITH THE ROMAN WOLF SUCKLING ROMULUS AND REMUS (0927)
Pen and brown wash, heightened with white, on blue paper.
394×282 mm.; 15½×11⅛ in.
Provenance: General John Guise.
Literature: Bell, cc.7^B (as by Paolo Farinati); J. A. Gere in *Master Drawings*, I, 1963, p. 17, No. 35.

Drawings in the Graphische Sammlung, Munich, for the frescoes by Trometta in the choir of S. Maria in Aracoeli, Rome (1566–

68), were first recognized by Hermann Voss (*Zeichnungen der italienischen Spätrenaissance*, 1928); to these and one or two other attributions by Voss, Mr. Gere (*loc. cit.*) has added a considerable number, including further studies for the Aracoeli frescoes. Gere has skilfully defined the style of this able follower (perhaps pupil) of Taddeo Zuccaro, whose work has been scantily noticed before.

Gere supposes that this is a part-study for the decoration of a façade, and that the blank space is a window. Bell in his Handlist describes it as a doorway, but it is hardly conceivable that the artist should have produced so top-heavy a design for a whole wall, even though some lack of balance in ornamental detail is often characteristic of Trometta, as Gere himself observes (*loc. cit.*, pp. 10–11). The two panels to right and left of the opening do not correspond in design, and the drawing was no doubt intended to offer alternative schemes of decoration here. In spite of the defect referred to, it is one of the best in quality of Trometta's drawings.

Tuscan (?) School
Second half of XIV century

75 *Recto*: THREE APOSTLES(?)
STANDING
Verso: INTERIOR OF A
GOTHIC CHAPEL, WITH A
HANGING LANTERN (0001)
Pen and brown ink and grey-brown wash, heightened with white body color, on pink grounded paper. The *verso* drawn entirely (?) with the brush.
185 × 199 mm.; 7⅚₆ × 7¹³⁄₁₆ in.
Provenance: Ridolfi; General John Guise.
Literature: Bell, A.1; B. Degenhart in

Münchner Jahrbuch, 1, 1950, p. 121; Degenhart and Schmitt, *Corpus der Italienischen Zeichnungen, 1300–1450*, 1, 1968, No. 164.
Exhibited: Matthiesen, 1960, No. 75.

Dr. Bernhard Degenhart and Dr. Annegrit Schmitt consider this to be near in style to Cenno di Francesco Cenni, a pupil of Agnolo Gaddi, by whom there are extensive frescoes in the church of S. Francesco at Volterra. Regarding the *verso*, they make the interesting observation that similar hanging lanterns appear in two of Giotto's frescoes in the Upper Church at Assisi—the *Vision of the Thrones* and the *Confirmation of the Stigmata in the Body of St. Francis*.

Cenni's types are provincial and conventionalized; the heads in the Christ Church drawing seem to me much more individual, and the figures more solidly conceived. It may be worth considering whether the drawing is necessarily Tuscan, rather than North Italian of the school of Verona or Padua, where the architecture and the Giottesque influence would be equally appropriate. In any case I suspect that the date (early XV century) suggested by Degenhart and Schmitt may be a little too late.

Tuscan School
Second half of XV century

76 BUST OF A MONK, FULL
FACE (0003)
Pen and brush, with watercolor and body color, over traces of black chalk. A fragment (222 × 178 mm.; 8¾ × 7 in., max.) laid down and matted to rectangular shape.
226 × 181 mm.; 8⅞ × 7⅛ in.
Provenance: General John Guise.
Literature: Bell, A.3 (as Italian School,

1400–1500); J. Q. van Regteren Altena in *Master Drawings*, VIII, 1970, p. 401 and Pl. 38 (as perhaps by Benozzo Gozzoli).

The drawing, apparently only a fragment of what may have been a half-length or even whole-length figure, is of remarkable quality, bold and sensitive in execution, and vivid in expression. It looks like a portrait from life, and has been supposed to represent S. Bernardino (d. 1440) or his disciple S. Giovanni Capistrano (d. 1456), to both of whom there is some resemblance; but neither identification is absolutely convincing, and the drawing might not be earlier than *c.* 1470–80. Professor van Regteren Altena's suggestion, that this might be a late work of Gozzoli (1420–1497), deserves serious consideration.

Ascribed to Giovanni da Udine
1487–1561/64

77 STUDIES OF PIGEONS (0175)
Pen and watercolor.
252 × 175 mm.; 9$\frac{15}{16}$ × 6$\frac{7}{8}$ in.
Provenance: Salomon Gautier; General John Guise.
Literature: Bell, E.23.
Exhibited: Matthiesen, 1960, No. 28; Liverpool, 1964, No. 47.

The old attribution cannot be accepted as certain, and it was rejected by Mme Nicole Dacos, whose study of the grotteschi of the *Domus Aurea* and their influence on Renaissance artists was published by the Warburg Institute in 1969. Such drawings are commonly catalogued under Giovanni's name on account of the birds introduced by him into his decoration of the Vatican *Loggie*; but none has been quite certainly established as

directly connected with that work. The Christ Church drawing is lively and good, certainly not a copy; more sketchy and spontaneous than those more elaborate bird-studies in the Chatsworth Collection which are regarded as of Giovanni da Udine's circle (see cat. of the second Chatsworth Exhibition, U.S.A., 1969–70, Nos. 4 and 5), or the *Cock Pheasant* in the British Museum (Pouncey and Gere cat., No. 153).

Francesco Vanni
1563–1610

78 THE CANONIZATION OF ST. CATHERINE OF SIENA; WITH THE BEATO BERNARDO TOLOMEI AND THE BEATA NERA TOLOMEI IN THE FOREGROUND, LEFT AND RIGHT (0208)
Pen and brown wash over black chalk. Partly squared and marked for measurement round the margin.
261 × 271 mm.; 10$\frac{1}{4}$ × 10$\frac{11}{16}$ in.
Provenance: General John Guise.
Literature: Bell, F.21; J. Byam Shaw in *Album Amicorum J. G. van Gelder*, 1973.

Composition study for the fresco painted by Vanni in 1600 in the Oratorio di S. Caterina in Siena (Venturi, IX, 7, Fig. 590). The most striking difference between the drawing and the fresco is that in the drawing the catafalque is so placed that the new saint's body is sharply foreshortened, with the feet towards the spectator, whereas in the final solution she lies in profile, filling more of the central space.

The drawing is a document of great importance especially in view of the damaged condition of the fresco. For the derivation of the composition from Passignano's fresco of the *Funeral of St. Antoninus* in S. Marco, Florence (Venturi, IX, 7, Fig. 350), see my note to be published in *Album Amicorum J. G. van Gelder*, 1973. A small pen-and-wash sketch for the whole composition, again with the saint's body foreshortened, is in the communal library at Siena.

A close replica of the Christ Church drawing, known to me only from a photograph but apparently of good quality, was acquired in 1967 by the Museum of Montreal. It shows exactly the same differences from the fresco in Siena.

Giorgio Vasari
1511–1574

79 POPE LEO X IN PROCESSION, PASSING THROUGH THE PIAZZA DELLA SIGNORIA IN FLORENCE (0185)
Pen and brown wash over indications in rough black chalk. Squared for enlargement in black chalk.
310×454 mm.; 12 3/16 × 17 7/8 in.
Provenance: Salomon Gautier; General John Guise.
Literature: Bell, E.33; Catherine Monbeig-Goguel, *Il Manierismo Fiorentino*, 1971, p. 85 and Pl. XXVI.

An important working drawing for one of the wall-paintings in the Sala di Leone X in the Palazzo Vecchio, decorated by Vasari soon after 1558. The event here recorded occurred in 1515—the first visit of Leo X to his native city since his election to the papacy in 1513, when he was on his way to meet the French King Francis I at Bologna.

Between Palazzo Vecchio on the left and the Loggia dei Lanzi in the center, the drawing shows a vista of the river Arno, with the ancient church of San Piero Scheraggio and old houses still standing, all to be demolished very shortly after the drawing was done to make room for the palace of the Uffizi, which Vasari himself designed.

It is interesting to find that Vasari had introduced some anachronisms in the Christ Church drawing which he corrected in the painting. The *Perseus* of Benvenuto Cellini (in the left-hand arch of the Loggia) and the *Hercules and Cacus* of Bandinelli (in front of the Palazzo Vecchio next to Michelangelo's *David*) are here shown in the positions they occupied when Vasari undertook the decoration of the Quartiere di Leone X (1558); but neither work was in existence in 1515. Donatello's *Judith*, on the other hand, now in front of the Palazzo, is correctly shown as it was at the time, under the right arch of the Loggia.

For the painting and good historical notes, see Piero Bargellini, *Scoperta di Palazzo Vecchio*, 1968, p. 117. The painting follows the drawing closely in general composition; but whereas in the drawing the personages riding in the procession, in the lower left foreground, are all conventional types, in the painting the ranks are filled with portraits—Pietro Aretino, Ariosto, Lorenzo de' Medici, Giovanni dalle Bande Nere, and others—derived from earlier sources.

80 DUKE COSIMO I, ELEONORA OF TOLEDO HIS WIFE, AND FIVE OF THEIR SONS: probably Francesco (b. 1541), Giovanni (b. 1543), Pietro (b. 1546), Garzia (b. 1547), and Ferdinando (b. 1549) (0183)
Pen and brown wash.
283×210 mm.; 11 1/8 × 8 1/4 in.

Provenance: General John Guise.
Literature: Bell, E.31; G. Poggi in *Rivista d'Arte*, IX, 1916, p. 42 and plate; E. Kris, *Steinschneide-Kunst in der italienischen Renaissance*, Vienna, 1929, I, p. 171, No. 310, and text p. 79; Morassi, *Art Treasures of the Medici*, 1964, Pl. 25.

Both Poggi (*loc. cit.*) and Kris (*op. cit.*, No. 309) reproduce the important cameo in Florence, by Giovanni Antonio de' Rossi of Milan, for which this interesting drawing seems to be the original design; it is also reproduced, with the attribution to Pierino da Vinci, in Venturi, X, 2, p. 338, Fig. 293, and by Morassi, *loc. cit.*

Vasari (ed. Milanesi, V, p. 387) describes the cameo as the work of de' Rossi, but says that it contained the portraits of all Cosimo's children, whereas in fact the two daughters, Isabella (b. 1542) and Lucrezia (b. 1540) are not included either there or in the Christ Church drawing. It is strange that he should make this mistake; and even more so that he makes no mention of his own drawing. But whatever the explanation may be there can surely be no doubt that the drawing is in fact by him. From the apparent age of the children, one would guess the date to be *c.* 1552 (if the smallest is really Ferdinando, b. 1549); but it appears from documents published by Poggi (*loc. cit.*) that de' Rossi only arrived in Florence to work for Cosimo I at the beginning of 1557, that he was working on the cameo two years later, that he was still working on it in Rome in 1561, and that he had promised to finish it by June 1562. Probably it was never finished, for the medallion held by the Duke and Duchess, which was intended to contain a figure representing Florence ("una Fiorenza"), is blank, as it is in Vasari's drawing. The elabo-rate framework of the drawing, with the inscription above and the arms of Medici and Toledo below, may also never have been executed; the side-pieces and top corners of this are clearly intended as alternative designs.

Giovanni de' Vecchi
1537–1615

81 CHRIST IN GLORY, WITH THE VIRGIN AND ST. JOHN THE BAPTIST, SS. PETER AND PAUL, STEPHEN, AND LAWRENCE: design for an apse (1342)
Pen and brown wash and watercolor (pink, yellow, mauve) with body color, over black chalk.
387×490 mm.; $15\frac{1}{4} \times 19\frac{5}{16}$ in.
Provenance: The "double numbering" collector; General John Guise.
Literature: Bell, p. 83 (large portfolio) (as by Salimbeni); Myril Pouncey in *Master Drawings*, VI, 1968, p. 250 and Pl. 13.

Mrs. Pouncey reproduces (*loc. cit.*, Fig. 1) a drawing in the Uffizi of *Christ as Judge, with Angels rescuing Souls from Purgatory*, which is nearly related to ours in style, and tentatively suggests that the impressive Christ Church drawing may have been connected with Giovanni de' Vecchi's work in S. Lorenzo in Damaso, Rome.

Paolo Veronese (Paolo Caliari)
1528–1588

82 *Recto*: SKETCHES FOR THE CORONATION OF THE VIRGIN
Verso: ANOTHER SKETCH

FOR THE SAME; OTHERS
FOR AN ANNUNCIATION;
AND VARIOUS FIGURES
FOR SPANDRELS OR
PEDIMENTS (0341)
Pen and brown wash.
305 × 210 mm.; 12 × 8¼ in.
On the *recto* are numerous annotations
in the artist's hand, names of saints and
prophets to appear in the composition,
and others. On the *verso*, some nu-
merals also in Paolo's hand.
Provenance: Sir P. Lely (L.2092); Gen-
eral John Guise.
Literature: Bell, κ.18; D. von Hadeln,
*Venezianische Zeichnungen der Spätre-
naissance*, 1926, p. 31, Pls. 38, 39; G.
Fiocco, *Veronese*, 1928, p. 210; H. and
E. Tietze, *Drawings of the Venetian Paint-
ers*, 1944, No. 2128.
Exhibited: Venice, 1958, Fondazione
Giorgio Cini, *Disegni Veneti di Oxford*,
No. 41; Royal Academy, 1960, No. 565;
Matthiesen, 1960, No. 78; Liverpool,
1964, No. 49; Venice, 1971, Fonda-
zione Giorgio Cini, *Disegni Veronesi del
Cinquecento*, No. 64.

A characteristic sheet of studies, mainly for
the *Coronation of the Virgin*, the altarpiece
painted for the church of Ognissanti *c.* 1586,
now in the Accademia, Venice (Venturi, IX,
4, Fig. 741, wrongly attributed to Monte-
mezzano). The *recto* is unusually pictorial in
effect, though it is in fact hardly more than a
conglomeration of notes for individual
groups in the composition. Many of the
saints named can be identified in the painting; and the group of the Coronation in the
center of the *recto*, as well as that on the *verso*,
has been followed rather closely. Other
studies for a Coronation, in exactly the same

late style but differently composed, are on a
sheet in Berlin (Hadeln, *op. cit.*, Pl. 40).

I cannot find any painting of the Annunciation to which the two little sketches on
the *verso* can be related. From the shape indicated, they might be an idea for the inner
sides of organ shutters. The figures reclining
on pediments, on the *verso* below, bear some
resemblance to the fresco fragments in the
Victoria and Albert Museum, London, to
which the catalogue of the Matthiesen Gallery exhibition (1960) drew attention; but
allegorical figures of this kind, decorating
pediments, are common in Veronese's work
at various periods.

83 ST. DOROTHY (1323)
Brush and brown wash over black
chalk, on blue paper.
405 × 242 mm.; 15¹⁵⁄₁₆ × 9½ in.
Provenance: possibly Jabach; Crozat;
General John Guise.
Literature: Not in Bell.

This important drawing, which has remained unnoticed in the Veronese literature,
and has only lately been mounted at Christ
Church, is certainly very close to the master
himself in style, though it is not in a technique usually associated with him. The facial
type, the graceful swaying movement, and
the full drapery are characteristic of Paolo at
a fairly early date, hardly before 1560, but not
long after that. The figure may be compared
with the women playing musical instruments on the walls of the *Sala a crociera* of the
Villa Barbaro at Maser, and with monochrome figures in painted niches in other
rooms of the same villa (1560–61) (Luciana
Crosato, *Gli Affreschi nelle Ville Venete*,
1962, Pls. 5, 6, 8, 10).

The naked child appears again, in the reverse direction, in a grisaille of *Charity* pub-

lished by Venturi in 1929 (*Storia*, IX, 4, p. 826 and Fig. 588).

Andrea del Verrocchio
1435–1488

84 HEAD OF A YOUNG
WOMAN, LOOKING DOWN
TO LEFT: a cartoon   (0005)
Black chalk, rubbed over, with a little body color, slightly touched in places with pen and ink. On two sheets, joined on the right. Pricked for transfer.
408×327 mm.; 16⅟₁₆×13⅞ in.
Provenance: General John Guise.
Literature: Bell, A.5; Berenson, 1938 and 1961 eds., No. 2782A (formerly No. 2800); Colvin, III, 1; van Marle, XI (1929), p. 534; Popham, *Italian Drawings*, 1931, No. 51; V. N. Gratchenkov, *Drawings of the Italian Renaissance*, Moscow, 1963 (in Russian), Pl. 29.
Exhibited: Royal Academy, 1930, No. 452; Paris, Petit Palais, 1935, No. 735; Royal Academy, 1953, No. 42; Matthiesen, 1960, No. 79; Liverpool, 1964, No. 50.

The drawing has been to some extent reworked (as Colvin was the first to notice), with left-handed hatchings apparently done with the point of the brush and light grey wash (in the shadow on temple, cheek, and throat). The *Head of an Angel looking down*, in the Uffizi (Popham, *op. cit.*, No. 53) is reworked in exactly the same way. Whether the penwork on the contours of nose, mouth, and chin is due to the artist is another question; it seems in some respects to correct the chalk lines underneath.

In spite of the retouching, the drawing is of great beauty, and fully worthy of Ver-

rocchio's own hand. The free chalk-work in hair, veil, and dress is of the finest quality, recalling Vasari's description of drawings by Verrocchio in his own collection: "*alcune teste di femina con bell'arie ed acconciature di capelli,*" which, says Vasari, inspired Leonardo.

Among paintings generally ascribed to Verrocchio, the closest relationship is perhaps to the *Virgin and Child* with a landscape background in Berlin (repr. Berenson, *Florentine Drawings*, 1961 ed., side by side with the Christ Church drawing).

Federico Zuccaro
1540/41–1609

85 DESIGN FOR THE DECORA-
TION OF THE CHOIR OF
THE CATHEDRAL OF
FLORENCE   (1389)
Pen and brown wash, over red chalk, on one sheet of paper of exceptional size.
518×480 mm.; 20⅜×18⅞ in.
Provenance: P. H. Lankrink (L.2090); General John Guise.
Literature: Bell, p. 93 (large portfolio); Detlev Heikamp in *Paragone*, 1967, No. 205 (March), p. 48 and Fig. 18.

This very important drawing is Federico's project for the decoration in fresco of the drum and one of the piers supporting the cupola of the Duomo—a project to be submitted to the Grand Duke Francesco I after the artist had completed, in October 1579, the decoration of the cupola itself. The Provveditore dell'Opera del Duomo, Benedetto Busini, protested to the Grand Duke about the probable expense, and the decoration was in fact never carried out.

Dr. Heikamp, in his very valuable account of Zuccaro's work in Florence between 1575 and 1579, draws attention to some interesting features of the Christ Church drawing. Between the arches is a *quadro riportato*, or feigned picture (frame and hooks complete), the subject of which is described by Heikamp as *Christ and the Seventy Preachers*, but is rather *The Deeds of Antichrist*: it derives in general idea, and in some details, from one of Signorelli's famous frescoes at Orvieto, from which Federico Zuccaro made free copies in another drawing at Christ Church (inv. no. 0131). On the pier itself—the one which encloses the Sacristy—Zuccaro proposes to place the organ over the door, with a painted figure of *Musica* and the Medici arms above it. But it is intriguing to note that he takes no thought for the two famous *cantorie* of Donatello and Luca della Robbia, which are now in the Museo dell'Opera, but were in those days, and indeed until 1688, in their original place on that pier.

86 PORTA VIRTUTIS: ART TRIUMPHANT OVER IGNORANCE AND CALUMNY (0213)

Pen and brown wash, with some corrections in thick white body color. Squared for enlargement in red chalk. 378 × 276 mm.; $14\frac{7}{8} \times 10\frac{7}{8}$ in.
Inscribed by the artist with the names of the allegorical personages.
Provenance: General John Guise.
Literature: Bell, F.26; D. Heikamp in *Rivista d'Arte*, XXXIII, 1958, pp. 45–50; F. Stampfle and J. Bean in *The Italian Renaissance: Drawings from New York Collections*, 1965, under No. 141.
Exhibited: Matthiesen, 1960, No. 80.

This is the best of three drawings, all by Federico, of this celebrated allegory; it is a preliminary sketch for the large painted cartoon of this composition, which was exhibited by the artist against the façade of the church of S. Luca in Rome on St. Luke's day, October 18, 1581. It was the annual festival of the Virtuosi al Pantheon, a society of which Zuccaro was then Regent. The satire was thought to reflect upon members of the papal household, and so offended Pope Gregory XIII that Zuccaro and his assistant, Domenico Passignano, were brought to trial and summarily exiled from Rome (November 27, 1581). Zuccaro's plea (which was probably true) was that his satire was directed not at the papal household, but at the Florentines who had criticized his work in the cathedral of Florence (see No. 85 of this cat.), and at the ignorance and envy of critics in general. The evidence is printed in full in *Giornale di erudizione artistica*, v, 1876, pp. 129ff.

The painting was no doubt destroyed, but two other drawings exist in Frankfurt and in the collection of Mr. János Scholz in New York. The Christ Church drawing is rougher and more spontaneous, with *pentimenti* in the figures and with some of the inscriptions carelessly scribbled in (*e.g.*, *porta virtus* for *porta virtutis* over the arch). All these irregularities are tidied up in the other versions, which may be regarded as "fair copies" by the artist himself.

The figures $42\frac{3}{4}$ scribbled vertically across the breast of *Invidia* (below center) might be an indication of the height intended for the painting. If so, and if the measurement is in *palmi romani* (1 *palmo* = 22.3 cm.), it must have been very large indeed.

I am much indebted to Mr. John Gere for

showing me his notes on the *Porta Virtutis*, which have enabled me to correct some misstatements in the previous literature.

Taddeo Zuccaro
1529–1566

87 STUDY FOR THE LEFT HALF OF AN *ADORATION OF THE SHEPHERDS*: a group of shepherds adoring, with the Virgin Mary at top right   (1420)
Pen and brown wash over rough black chalk, in parts heightened with body color, on four pieces of paper joined and toned yellowish brown.
437×672 mm.; 17 3/16 × 26 7/16 in.
Provenance: Sir P. Lely (L.2092); General John Guise.
Literature: Not in Bell; J. Gere, *Taddeo Zuccaro*, 1970, pp. 68–69, 186, No. 167 and Pl. 51.

Mr. Gere plausibly connects this splendid drawing with one in the Royal Library at Windsor (Popham and Wilde cat. no. 1078 and Pl. 89) which is of similarly large dimensions, on paper toned the same color, and represents a group of shepherds and St. Joseph facing left, obviously for the right half of the same subject. Comparable or related drawings are also at Chatsworth (Gere, cat. 18, 19). All these drawings Gere supposes may have been done in connection with the decoration of the Mattei Chapel in S. Maria della Consolazione, Rome, begun in 1553 and finished in 1556.

88 *Recto*: ALEXANDER AND BUCEPHALUS
Verso: SKETCHES FOR A BASAMENTO   (0177)
Pen and bistre wash, over indications in black chalk.
376×429 mm.; 14 13/16 × 16 7/8 in.
Provenance: General John Guise.
Literature: Bell, E.25; J. Gere, *Taddeo Zuccaro*, 1970, pp. 71, 185, No. 162, and Pls. 41, 42.

The subject of this brilliant drawing recalls scenes from the life of Alexander the Great painted in fresco by Taddeo in the Castello Odescalchi at Bracciano (Gere, *op. cit.*, Pls. 122 and 123) and in Palazzo Caetani in Rome (*ibid.*, Pls. 124–129); but those decorations are of 1559–60, and the present drawing is certainly earlier. Mr. Gere dates it early in the 1550s, and tentatively connects the *verso* with the decoration of the Mattei Chapel in S. Maria della Consolazione in Rome (1553–56). Very similar decoration, apparently intended to be carried out in stucco below the main subjects, appears in a more elaborate drawing for that project in Mr. Gere's own collection (*op. cit.*, No. 121 and Pl. 43).

Jacopo Zucchi
c. 1542–1589/90

89 DESIGN FOR A CHAPEL, WITH AN ALTARPIECE OF THE ADORATION OF THE MAGI   (0983)
Pen and brown wash over black chalk.
360×277 mm.; 14 3/16 × 10 15/16 in.
Inscribed with texts from the Prophets, etc., in the artist's hand.
Provenance: General John Guise.
Literature: Bell, DD.16 (as by Boscoli).

Mr. Pouncey's attribution of this excellent and important *modello* seems absolutely convincing. The style reflects the influence of both Francesco Salviati and Vasari. Much of the decoration (some of it remarkably profane) was probably intended to be carried out in stucco. Mr. Edmund Pillsbury has observed that the style of the architectural parts resembles that of the Tulfia Chapel in S. Spirito in Sassia, Rome (first chapel on right), which was decorated by Zucchi in 1588–89.

II · NON-ITALIAN SCHOOLS

Dutch and Flemish Schools

Abraham Bloemaert
1564–1651

90 THE MASS OF ST. GREGORY (1328)
Pen and brown wash over black chalk, heightened with white body color, on coarse buff paper, squared for transfer and indented with the stilus.
467 × 373 mm.; 18⅜ × 14¹¹⁄₁₆ in.
Provenance: General John Guise.
Literature: Not in Bell; C. J. White in *Master Drawings*, VI, 1968, p. 257 and Pl. 19.

A drawing of unusual size and importance, evidently intended for engraving, though no such print is recorded.

91 *Recto*: TWO STUDIES OF THE HEAD OF A YOUNG MAN; AND A RIGHT HAND HOLDING AN OPEN BOOK
Verso: STUDIES OF HEADS, ARMS AND A LEG, AND THE HEAD AND SHOULDERS OF A RECUMBENT MAN (0493)

Red and white chalk, slightly touched with the pen, on coarse buff paper. Corners cut.
270 × 330 mm.; 10⅝ × 13 in. (max.)
Provenance: General John Guise.
Literature: Bell, 0.25 (as by Ludovico Carracci); C. J. White in *Master Drawings*, VI, 1968, p. 258 and Pls. 23, 24.
Exhibited: Royal Academy, 1938, No. 369 (as by Ludovico Carracci); Matthiesen, 1960, No. 4; Liverpool, 1964, No. 2.

The old attribution to Ludovico Carracci was accepted by Bodmer. The drawing is, however, absolutely characteristic of Bloemaert and a very fine example. Dr. Christopher White (*loc. cit.*) draws attention to the relationship of some of the studies on the *verso* to those in Bloemaert's *Tekenboek*, engraved by his son Frederick.

Anthonie van Borssom
1630–1677

92 A WATERMEADOW WITH CATTLE, ON THE OUTSKIRTS OF A TOWN (1129)
Pen and brown and green watercolor over black lead or chalk; the distance unfinished.

238 × 365 mm.; 9⅜ × 14⅜ in.
Provenance: General John Guise.
Literature: Bell, HH.24.

Entirely characteristic of Borssom in subject, in handling of the pen, and in the watercolor washes. Professor J. Q. van Regteren Altena suggests that the view may be the dyke of the Zuiderzee looking towards Morraikendam. The building lightly indicated in the distance right center seems to be a castle with a tower.

Leonard Bramer
1596–1674

93 *Recto*: SOLDIERS BEHIND A BALUSTRADE
Verso: A SIMILAR GROUP (0789)
Brush and grey wash with a little white body color on buff paper.
389 × 294 mm.; 15 5/16 × 11 9/16 in.
Provenance: General John Guise.
Literature: Bell, X.18 (as Italian, 1700–1725).
Exhibited: Matthiesen, 1960, No. 6; Liverpool, 1964, No. 4.

Typical of Bramer's highly original manner of drawing with the brush, but of unusual scale and importance. The artist was in Italy 1616–28, and drawings of this sort show something of the influence of the followers of Caravaggio.

A similar group of figures appeared high on the wall of the Prinsenhof hall at Delft, which was decorated by Bramer in 1668. The paintings have been destroyed, but a drawing by A. Terwesten (1743) shows the scheme (see Wichmann, *Leonaert Bramer*, 1923, Pl. XXXI).

Bartholomäus Breenbergh
1599–1657

94 *Recto*: ROMAN RUINS (the Baths of Caracalla ?)
Verso: RUINS OF A ROMAN GATE (1062)
Pen and bistre wash, over black chalk.
245 × 403 mm.; 9⅝ × 15⅞ in.
There is a contemporary inscription in Dutch on the *verso*, apparently giving the locality.
Provenance: General John Guise.
Literature: Bell, FF.19 (as by Claude).

A fine example of Breenbergh's Italian style, dating from the 1620s; but not included in Röthlisberger, *Breenbergh Handzeichnungen*, 1969.

Dutch School
c. 1520–1530

95 *Recto*: A MAN SEATED (DRAWING?) ON A THREE-LEGGED STOOL, AMONG ANTIQUE RUINS
Verso: STUDIES OF DONKEYS (0297)
Recto, pen and brown ink; *verso*, black chalk (with some rubbing of red chalk from other sheets).
202 × 127 mm.; 7 15/16 × 5 in.
Provenance: Ridolfi; General John Guise.
Literature: Bell, I.1 (as by Catena).

This interesting study was considered by Mr. A. E. Popham to be very close in style to Pieter Cornelisz. Kunst (c. 1490–c. 1540). The style of his most familiar drawings, of which many exist, is more related to that of the fashionable Antwerp Mannerists of the 1520s and 30s; they show too a Düreresque calligraphy in the penwork, which I miss in the Christ Church drawing. Here there is no trace of Mannerism, and the shading is loosely scribbled or hatched. The figure, obviously sketched from life, has the sort of realism that reminds me of the *naar het leven* studies of peasants generally attributed to Pieter Bruegel the elder; and indeed the animal-studies on the *verso* are not unlike Bruegel's. But I do not suggest that our drawing is by him.

Sir Anthony Van Dyck
1599–1641

96 PORTRAIT OF JUSTIN VAN MEERSTRATEN (1092)
Black chalk with a little white chalk on blue paper.
338 × 226 mm.; 13 5/16 × 8 7/8 in.
Provenance: General John Guise.
Literature: Bell, GG.14; Colvin, III, 22; G. Glück, *Van Dyck (Klassiker der Kunst)*, 1933, under No. 416.
Exhibited: Royal Academy, 1938, No. 615; Matthiesen, 1960, No. 19; Liverpool, 1964, No. 13.

Study for the portrait in the Cassel Gallery, dated by Glück *c.* 1634–35.

Jakob de Gheyn II
1565–1629

97 A WITCHES' SABBATH (1083–1084)
Pen and brown ink and grey wash; with a little heightening in body color, on buff paper.
377 × 519 mm.; 14 13/16 × 20 7/16 in.
Signed *I. D. Gheyn* (initial letters in monogram) on a separate piece of paper attached below center.

Provenance: General John Guise.
Literature: Bell, GG.7–8; J. Q. van Regteren Altena, *The Drawings of Jacques de Gheyn*, 1936, p. 45.
Exhibited: Matthiesen, 1960, Nos. 23–24.

This very remarkable drawing, so characteristic of de Gheyn in subject but of unusual size and importance, was cut in two at an early date, and the two halves remained mounted separately until 1969. Professor van Regteren Altena, however, had already noticed, more than forty years ago, that the compositions are contiguous; in fact they fit exactly together on the central vertical line. Probably a strip has been cut away at the bottom, from which the signature, which is now attached at lower center, was salvaged.

Similar scenes of witchcraft are among the drawings by de Gheyn in Berlin (No. 3205) and in the Ashmolean Museum (Parker, I, p. 37, Pl. IX); an engraved composition of the same kind, after his design, was published by N. de Clerck (Hollstein 96). The Ashmolean drawing, also a very fine example, is indistinctly dated, probably 1600.

Hugo van der Goes
d. 1482

98 JACOB AND RACHEL (1335)
Point of the brush (some penwork, perhaps, in some of the faces) and brown wash, heightened with white body color, on slate-grey prepared paper. Patched at upper left corner with three or four small strips (possibly by the artist).
336 × 571 mm.; 13 1/4 × 22 1/2 in.
Provenance: General John Guise.
Literature: Bell, H.87; Colvin, III, 17; J. Destrée, *Hugo van der Goes*, 1914, p. 74

(repr.); L. von Baldass in *Mitteilungen der Gesellschaft für vervielfältigende Kunst*, 1919, p. 2; Kurt Pfister, *Van der Goes*, 1923, Pl. 36; M. J. Friedländer, *Altniederländische Malerei*, IV, 1924, p. 62 and Pl. LXXVI; A. E. Popham, *Drawings of the Early Flemish School*, 1926, p. 26 and Pls. 23, 24; V. Denis, *Hugo van der Goes*, 1956, p. 21; O. Benesch in *Jahrbuch der Kunsthistorischen Sammlungen in Wien*, LIII, 1957, pp. 11ff.; [A. Seilern], *Flemish Paintings and Drawings at 56 Princes Gate*, IV, Addenda, 1969, p. 40 and Figs. 45–47; F. Winkler, *Van der Goes*, 1964, p. 267 and Fig. 176.

Exhibited: Royal Academy, 1927, No. 505; Royal Academy, 1953, No. 240; Matthiesen, 1960, No. 29; Liverpool, 1964, No. 16.

Most critics who have had the opportunity of studying the original will agree with Count Antoine Seilern's warm appreciation of this beautiful drawing, which he reproduces (with two excellent details) in support of the attribution to Van der Goes of the *Saint* in his own collection (*op. cit.*, Pls. XXVI, XXVII). I was able to examine Count Seilern's drawing side by side with that at Christ Church, and can only confirm his statement that the two are quite certainly by the same hand.

Seilern's defence of the Christ Church drawing against the strictures of Friedländer, Baldass, and Winkler (and also of the cataloguer of the Matthiesen Gallery exhibition of 1960) is also admirable. Friedländer and Winkler both considered the drawing original, but to some extent retouched by a later hand, especially in the background; Baldass considered the whole to be a copy of the XVI century, but this is emphatically denied

by Popham. I see none of the weaknesses suggested by these writers: the drawing of detail—the hands and feet particularly—is of the highest order; and as for the landscape, which is rather more roughly drawn, the slender trees and wooded hills are perfectly in character with those in the right wing of the Portinari altarpiece, or the *Adam and Eve* in Vienna, and make exactly the right foil to the figures. The fact that the small figure of a herdsman in the middle distance left center is clearly drawn *over* the horizontal line of the landscape seems also to refute the suggestion that the landscape is a later addition. The types of the shepherds are exactly those of the Portinari *Adoration*. This is in fact the most important surviving drawing by the master, of exceptional size and in excellent condition.

Jacob Jordaens
1593–1678

99 BUST OF A WOMAN WEARING A CAP AND RUFF, THREE-QUARTERS TO LEFT (1091)
Black and white chalks on buff paper. 337 × 273 mm.; 13¼ × 10¾ in.
Provenance: P. H. Lankrink (L.2090); General John Guise.
Literature: Bell, GG.13 (as School of Rubens).

The attribution to Jordaens, first made by J. C. Robinson, is surely correct.

Jan Lievens
1607–1674

100 FARM BUILDINGS AMONG TREES (1130)
Pen and brown ink.

203 × 306 mm.; 8 × 12 in.
Inscribed on the *verso* in red chalk:
L.1–10 and *p(?) de Widt.* Also *A no. 41*
in pen and ink.
Provenance: General John Guise.
Literature: Bell, HH.25.
Exhibited: Matthiesen, 1960, No. 41;
Liverpool, 1964, No. 25.

The name on the back may be that of Pieter
de With, a pupil of Rembrandt, who drew
somewhat in Lievens' manner. The figures
L.1–10 are probably a price-mark. The
drawing is certainly by Lievens, but may
have been bought by de With.

The author of the Matthiesen exhibition
catalogue of 1960 detects here the influence
of Rubens and Brouwer, and supposes the
drawing to be of Lievens' Antwerp period,
1635–43.

Rembrandt van Rijn
1606–1669

101 A NUDE WOMAN KNEEL-
ING ON A BED, HOLDING
A STICK (1127)
Pen and brown ink and wash.
225 × 148 mm.; 8⅞ × 5¹³⁄₁₆ in.
Provenance: M. (stamped blind, lower
left corner) (L.1842 and Suppl., p. 263;
probably Dutch, early XVIII century);
General John Guise.
Literature: Bell, HH.22; Colvin, III, 26;
R. Graul, *Fünfzig Zeichnungen von
Rembrandt*, 1906, Pl. 41; Benesch, Cor-
pus, 1957, V, No. 1116 and Fig. 1338.
Exhibited: Royal Academy, 1938, No.
561; Matthiesen, 1960, No. 63; Liver-
pool, 1964, No. 40.

Though somewhat faded and damaged, this
is still a fine example of a nude study by

Rembrandt, probably made *c.* 1655–60.
Benesch compares the drawing in Amsterdam, B.1117. The Chicago nude, B.1127,
is even closer in style. These and several
others (Munich, British Museum, etc.) are
surely from the same model.

Sir Peter Paul Rubens
1577–1640

102 FOUR PUTTI PLAYING ON
A GRAPE-VINE (1085)
Point of the brush, fine pen, brown
wash and white oil-paint, on buff pa-
per.
177 × 355 mm.; 7 × 14 in.
Provenance: P. H. Lankrink (L.2090);
John Talman (his border); General
John Guise.
Literature: Bell, GG.9; L. Burchard and
J. d'Hulst, catalogue of Antwerp ex-
hibition, 1956, under No. 119.
Exhibited: Antwerp, 1956, *Tekeningen
van P. P. Rubens*, No. 119; Matthiesen,
1960, No. 68.

Dated by Burchard and d'Hulst *c.* 1630, and
supposed by them to be a design for a decorative relief on a choir-screen or stall.

103 THE HEAD OF THE
EMPEROR GALBA, FORE-
SHORTENED: FROM AN
ANTIQUE BUST (1087)
Black chalk, heightened with white,
on pale buff paper.
377 × 277 mm.; 14¹³⁄₁₆ × 10¹⁵⁄₁₆ in.
Provenance: P. H. Lankrink (L.2090);
General John Guise.
Literature: Bell, GG.11; Waagen, 1854,
III, 49; Passavant, *Tour*, II, 140; L.
Burchard and J. d'Hulst, catalogue of
Antwerp exhibition, 1956, under No.
15; M. Jaffé, *Van Dyck's Antwerp*

Sketchbook, 1966, I, pp. 26–27 and Pl. XXXVII.

Exhibited: Antwerp, 1956, *Tekeningen van P. P. Rubens*, No. 15; Matthiesen, 1960, No. 66; Liverpool, 1964, No. 43.

The same bust in a less foreshortened view was etched by J. Episcopius (Jan de Bisschop) in *Paradigmata Graphices*, 1671, Pl. 54, with the inscription: *Galba, ex marmore antiq.* Another drawing of the same by Rubens was engraved by P. Aveline, *Théorie de la Figure Humaine . . .* , Paris, 1773, Pl. III. The bust appears in the background of Rubens' drawing of *Seneca* in the Hermitage.

104 MARS: TWO STUDIES FROM A SCULPTURED FIGURE (1171)

Oil-color, monochrome, on paper.
327 × 220 mm.; $14\frac{7}{8} \times 8\frac{5}{8}$ in.
Provenance: General John Guise.
Literature: Not in Bell.

The drawing has never been noticed or published. The figure is certainly connected with the famous statue of Mars Ultor, once in the cell of the temple of that divinity in the Forum of Augustus in Rome. There are many derivatives; a colossal marble is in the Capitoline museum (Bocconi, *The Capitoline Collections*, 1950, p. 65, No. 16). Rubens' model may have been a much smaller bronze.

German and Swiss Schools

Albrecht Dürer
1471–1528

105 STUDY FOR THE TOMB OF A KNIGHT AND HIS LADY (1109)

Pen and brown ink.
259 × 179 mm.; $10\frac{3}{16} \times 7\frac{1}{16}$ in.
Provenance: General John Guise.
Literature: Bell, HH.4; Colvin, III, 8; Winkler, *Dürers Zeichnungen*, II, 1937, No. 489 (with all previous literature); H. and E. Tietze, *Dürer*, 1937–38, *Katalog*, II, 1, w.75; E. Panofsky, *Dürer*, 1945, II (Handlist), No. 1543.
Exhibited: Matthiesen Gallery, 1960, No. 17; Nuremberg, Dürer Exhibition, 1971, No. 704.

A fine example of Dürer's brilliant penmanship. The date cannot be later than 1510, since the female figure seems to have been used in Dürer's woodcut of that year, Bartsch 125, *The Beheading of St. John Baptist* (for the maidservant of Salome). Two copies exist, in Berlin and in the Uffizi, Florence (the latter with monogram and date 1517, both false). The superiority of the Christ Church version is now universally accepted, in spite of the strictures of H. and E. Tietze, who catalogue it as a studio production.

The composition was used for two sepulchral monuments cast in bronze in the studio of the Nuremberg sculptor Peter Vischer the elder—one for Count Hermann VIII von Henneberg (d. 1535) and his wife Elisabeth von Brandenburg (d. 1507) in the church at Römhild, the other for Count Eitel Friedrich II von Hohenzollern (d. 1512) and his wife Magdalena von Brandenburg (d. 1496) in the church at Hechingen. The Hechingen monument follows the drawing more closely than the other; but both show considerable variations.

Hans Holbein the elder

c. 1460–1524

106 TWO STUDIES OF THE HEAD OF A WOMAN, AND THREE OF HANDS (1107)
Silverpoint on grey prepared paper. Cut irregularly and laid down, top corners rounded.
146×211 mm.; 5¾×8⁵⁄₁₆ in. (max.)
Provenance: Padre Resta; John, Lord Somers (*c.9*); General John Guise.
Literature: Bell, HH.2; Colvin, III, 2.
Exhibited: Royal Academy, 1953, No. 237; Matthiesen Gallery, 1960, No. 34; Manchester, 1961, *German Art*, No. 69; Liverpool, 1964, No. 19; Augsburg, 1965, *Hans Holbein the Elder*, No. 107.

The catalogue of the Matthiesen Gallery exhibition of 1960 throws some doubt on the attribution to the elder Holbein (which was first made by J. C. Robinson), and quotes Dr. E. Schilling's suggestion that this drawing may be an early work of Leonhard Beck, who was in Holbein's studio at Augsburg *c.*1500. It seems to me, however, so close in style and quality to the numerous examples from the elder Holbein's sketchbooks in Berlin, Basle, and elsewhere that I prefer to retain the older attribution. Professor F. Winzinger, who studied the drawing at Oxford in 1968, agrees with this view; and the authors of the catalogue entry for the Augsburg exhibition of 1965 also seem inclined to accept it.

Daniel Lindtmayer

1552–c. 1607

107 DESIGN FOR A GLASS-PAINTING: A knight in armour and a landsknecht supporting a figure of Justice on a pedestal, with two shields below bearing the letters P and W; and above, William Tell shooting at the apple on his son's head (1121)
Pen and India ink. Marked for leading in red ink by the glassmaker.
418×320 mm.; 16⁷⁄₁₆×12⁵⁄₈ in.
Signed with monogram DLM and dated 1574 beneath the figure of Justice.
Provenance: General John Guise.
Literature: Bell, HH.16; Friedrich Thöne, *Daniel Lindtmayer*, Zürich, 1972, No. 51*a* and Fig. 63.

An important and characteristic example of a design for domestic glass-painting, a very popular art in Switzerland in the second half of the XVI century. The pilaster on the right is indicated in outline only, the artist evidently thinking that the executant craftsman could repeat the detail from the pilaster on the left.

Dr. Friedrich Thöne, who has kindly supplied information from his forthcoming book on Lindtmayer, identifies the shield on the left as that of the Basel family of Werdenberg; and refers to another illustration of the story of William Tell in a design for glass in the Kunsthaus at Zürich, dated 1578 (a copy of a lost original by Lindtmayer).

Georg Pencz

c. 1500–1550

108 DESIGN FOR AN ILLUSIONIST CEILING, SHOWING WORKMEN BUILDING AN UPPER STOREY (0964)
Pen and reddish brown wash on brownish toned paper.
238×150 mm.; 9³⁄₈×5⁷⁄₈ in.

Provenance: General John Guise.
Literature: Bell, cc.31 (as by Tommaso Sandrino); H. and E. Tietze in *Old Master Drawings*, xiv, 1939, p. 18.
Exhibited: Matthiesen, 1960, No. 55; Manchester, 1961, *German Art*, No. 137; Liverpool, 1964, No. 34.

As the Tietzes were the first to observe, this elaborate *jeu d'esprit* is of exactly the same sort as a drawing in the collection at University College, London, first published by E. Kris in 1932, and certainly by the same hand. Kris (*Mitteilungen der Gesellschaft für vervielfältigende Kunst*, 1923, p. 45, and 1932, p. 65) had drawn attention to the description in Sandrart's *Teutsche Akademie* (1675) of a ceiling painted by Georg Pencz in the garden pavilion of Herr Volkamer's house in Nuremberg: a description that fits rather closely the drawing at University College, as well as that at Christ Church. Other similar drawings by Pencz are in the Albertina and the Louvre.

Pencz, who started his career as a pupil of Dürer, and was one of the most accomplished engravers among the so-called "little masters" of Nuremberg, later travelled through Italy to Rome, and it is suggested that these illusionist designs for ceiling-painting may have been inspired by what he saw, perhaps, of Mantegna in the castle at Mantua. The date of the Volkamer ceiling-painting is not known, but is likely to have been fairly late in the artist's career.

French School

Claude Gellée, called Le Lorrain
1600–1682

109 ROCKY LANDSCAPE, WITH TWO LARGE TREES, AND A VIEW OF THE SEA TO THE RIGHT (1064)
Pen and brown wash over black chalk. 183 × 132 mm.; 7$\frac{3}{16}$ × 5$\frac{3}{16}$ in.
Provenance: General John Guise.
Literature: Bell, FF.21; Vasari Society, 1st Series, x, 1914, p. 26; M. Röthlisberger, *Claude: The Drawings*, 1966, No. 486.
Exhibited: Paris, 1925, *Le Paysage Français de Poussin à Corot*, No. 465; Royal Academy, 1938, No. 533.

Dated by Röthlisberger 1640–45.

110 *Recto*: A RIVER IN FLOOD
Verso: A GROUP OF FIGURES STANDING AND KNEELING BY AN ALTAR (?) (1060)
The *recto* in pen and brush and brown wash over black lead or chalk; the *verso* in red chalk (much stained). 230 × 341 mm.; 9$\frac{1}{16}$ × 13$\frac{7}{16}$ in.
Provenance: General John Guise.
Literature: Bell, FF.17; Colvin, iii, 36; Hind, *The Drawings of Claude Lorrain*, 1925, Pl. 47; M. Röthlisberger, *Claude: The Drawings*, 1966, under No. 486.
Exhibited: Royal Academy, 1938, No. 516; Royal Academy, 1949, No. 464; Royal Academy, 1953, No. 378; Matthiesen, 1960, No. 9; Liverpool, 1964, No. 6.

The attribution to Claude dates only from the beginning of the present century, and doubts were expressed in the catalogue of the Royal Academy exhibition of 1938; but since then it has been generally accepted, except by Dr. Röthlisberger, who calls it "of the circle of Breenbergh-Swanevelt." In view of the early ascription to Rembrandt (on the old mounting-paper), the possibility that the drawing is by a Dutchman ought not to be disregarded entirely. On the other hand it is surely by an artist of great distinction, and the handling and color of the wash, the effect of distance, and the lighting are so much in character with Claude's studies from nature that I am inclined to keep the attribution to him. Both Mr. Michael Kitson (who suggests a date 1630–35) and Sir Anthony Blunt support this view.

The rough sketch on the *verso* is certainly surprising, but even here I do not share Dr. Röthlisberger's absolute conviction that it cannot be by Claude.

French School (the Master of the Parement de Narbonne)
Late XIV century

111 AN ARCHER DRAWING HIS BOW (0002)
Point of the brush on vellum. Cut irregularly and laid down. The ruler has been used for the bow-string and the arrow, and these lines only seem to be drawn with the pen.
267 × 160 mm.; 10½ × 6 5/16 in. (max.)
Provenance: Ridolfi; General John Guise.
Literature: Bell, A.2 (as Sienese School, XIV century); Grosvenor Gallery Photographs, No. 32; Colvin, II, 1; Otto Pächt in *Burlington Magazine*, XCVIII, 1956, p. 150; Millard Meiss, *French Painting in the Time of Jean de Berry: the late XIV Century*, 1967, p. 132 and Fig. 569.
Exhibited: Royal Academy, 1930, No. 415 (as Sienese, XIV century); Royal

Academy, 1953, No. 5; Matthiesen, 1960, No. 21; Liverpool, 1964, No. 14.

This extremely important and beautiful drawing, curiously suggestive of some Assyrian relief-carving, was attributed by Ridolfi (on a label below the present mount) to a certain Pace da Faenza, who is mentioned by Vasari (ed. Milanesi, I, p. 405) as a good disciple of Giotto and the author of paintings in Bologna, Forlì, and Assisi. Nothing of his can now be identified; and the drawing was simply classified as Sienese XIV century, until Dr. Otto Pächt made the interesting suggestion (already referred to in the catalogue of the Royal Academy Exhibition of 1953, but published only in 1956) that the draughtsman may have been the Master of the Parement de Narbonne, the painter of the celebrated altar-frontal of 1374 now in the Louvre.

In spite of the objections of Professor Meiss (*loc. cit.*), who considers the drawing to be Bohemian of about the same date, I find Dr. Pächt's attribution perfectly convincing; for my part I could not hope to find closer resemblances than those between this Archer and the figures of the executioners in the *Parement* itself. For excellent reproductions of the latter, see Meiss, *op. cit.*, Figs. 1–5.

Follower of Nicolas Poussin
(Nicolas Poussin, 1594–1665)

112 A VIEW OF S. GIORGIO IN VELABRO, ROME (1050)
Pen and brown and grey wash, over black chalk, on greenish grey ground, heightened with white body color.
180 × 301 mm.; 7⅛ × 11⅞ in.
Inscribed *N. Poussin* in pen and ink (XVII century?) on the drawing lower left center.

Provenance: General John Guise.
Literature: Bell, FF.8 (as by Nicolas Poussin); Colvin, 1907, III, 34; A. M. Hind in *Burlington Magazine*, XLVIII, 1926, pp. 192–195.
Exhibited: Royal Academy, 1938, No. 521 (as Nicolas Poussin); Royal Academy, 1949, No. 387 (as by an artist working in Rome under the influence of Poussin and Claude); Montreal, 1953, No. 157 (as Nicolas Poussin); Matthiesen, 1960, No. 16 (as by Gaspard Dughet); Liverpool, 1964, No. 11 (the same).

In spite of various other opinions that have been expressed since the drawings were exhibited in 1938, I still feel that this and No. 113 are nearer in style to Nicolas Poussin than to Dughet or any other artist known to me, and that they are by a very good hand. The attribution of our drawings to Dughet was suggested by Sir Anthony Blunt, but he no longer wishes to maintain it. He is convinced that the drawings are not by Nicolas Poussin.

The view is from the south, from the right-hand side of the Arch of Janus, which, curiously enough, the artist has introduced *behind* the church, below the tower of the Palazzo Senatorio. In the background, left center, to the right of the campanile of S. Giorgio in Velabro, can be recognized the church of S. Maria d' Aracoeli, and in front of that is what appears to be the church of S. Maria della Consolazione, with its façade still unfinished.

Poussin seems to have adapted the same buildings for the background of his *Christ healing the Blind* of 1650, now in the Louvre (Blunt, *Nicolas Poussin*, 1967, Pl. 201).

113 A VIEW OF THE AVENTINE HILL AND THE TIBER, ROME (1051)
Pen and brown wash, over black chalk, heightened with white body color, on greenish grey ground.
180 × 300 mm.; $7\frac{1}{8} \times 11\frac{13}{16}$ in.
Inscribed *N. Poussin* in pen and ink on the drawing, in a XVII-century (?) hand.
Provenance: General John Guise.
Literature: Bell, FF.9 (as by Nicolas Poussin); A. M. Hind in *Burlington Magazine*, XLVIII, 1926, p. 195.
Exhibited: Royal Academy, 1938, No. 525; Royal Academy, 1949, No. 392.

See note to No. 112 which is certainly by the same hand as this, though rather better.

The view is taken from the northwest, apparently from across the Tiber. Prominent on the extreme left of the top of the hill is the ancient church of S. Sabina, and in the middle the campanile of S. Alessio. Further to the right is a building apparently without windows, which seems to be the old chapel of the Priorato di Malta, afterwards rebuilt by Piranesi.

The view of the Aventine in the Uffizi, by Poussin himself, provides an interesting comparison (Friedländer-Blunt, IV, 1963, p. 45, No. 277, Pl. 216).

English School

Francis Barlow
1626–1702

114 THREE SQUIRRELS (1135)
Pen and brown ink, with grey wash, on white paper. Indented for engraving.

130 × 180 mm.; 5⅛ × 7⅛ in.
Signed below center: *F. Barlow.*
Provenance: Henry Aldrich, Dean of
Christ Church (d. 1710) (MS. Inventory of Aldrich Collection at Christ
Church, vol. H. 2, 60).
Literature: Bell, HH.29^A (a); John
Woodward, *Tudor and Stuart Drawings,* 1951, p. 48 and Pl. 26.

Etched with variations by Jan Griffier for the
series *Various Birds and Beasts,* with the inscription: *I. Griffier fecit, P. Tempest exc.* This
and No. 115 are excellent examples of Barlow's work as an illustrator of animal subjects. For others see Woodward, *op. cit.,* Pls.
27–32.

115 TWO HOUNDS HUNTING A HARE (1136)
Pen and brown ink, with grey wash,
on buff paper, heightened with white
body color. Indented for engraving.
128 × 181 mm.; 5⁄16 × 7⅛ in.
Signed and dated lower left: *F. Barlow*
[16]84.
Provenance: Henry Aldrich, Dean of
Christ Church (MS. Inventory of Aldrich Collection, vol. H. 2, 59).
Literature: Bell, HH.29^A (b).

Etched in reverse by Jan Griffier in the series
of *Various Birds and Beasts,* with the inscription: *F. Barlow delin. I. Griffier fecit. P. Tempest ex: 5.*

Inigo Jones
1573–1652

116 STUDIES OF HEADS, LEGS AND TORSO OF A MAN (0796)

Pen and dark brown ink.
270 × 187 mm.; 10⅝ × 7⅜ in.
Provenance: General John Guise.
Literature: Bell, X.25 (as Italian, 1600–
1650).

Clearly by Inigo Jones, and exactly in the
style of the sketches in his Roman notebook
of 1614. Many of these are inscribed by him
as copies of drawings or prints by or after
Italian artists of the High Renaissance—
Parmigianino, Polidoro, Raphael, Michelangelo, Schiavone, etc. Several of the heads
in the Christ Church drawing are reminiscent of Parmigianino, but I have failed to
identify any such sources. On the Roman
notebook, now at Chatsworth, see Roy
Strong's catalogue of the exhibition, *Festival
Designs by Inigo Jones,* circulated in U.S.A.
by the International Exhibitions Foundation, 1967–68, under No. 41. Jones travelled
to Italy, possibly for the second time, in
1613–15, in the train of Thomas, Earl of
Arundel.

117 STUDY OF THREE MALE HEADS (0497)
Pen and brown ink.
186 × 155 mm.; 7⁵⁄16 × 6⅛ in.
Provenance: General John Guise.
Literature: Bell, O.29 (as attributed to
Ludovico Carracci).

Though the drawing appears in C. F. Bell's
Handlist of 1914 under the name of Carracci,
it was he who subsequently suggested the
attribution to Inigo Jones, which is clearly
correct. Very similar heads, sometimes copied
from earlier Italian masters, occur in Jones's
Roman notebook of 1614, now at Chatsworth.

Spanish School

Jusepe de Ribera
c. 1590–1652

118   A WOMAN LOOKING
DOWN, HOLDING AN
ARROW   (1074)
Red chalk, heightened with white, on
buff paper.
310×206 mm.; 12⅜×8⅛ in.
Signed upper right: *Joseph à Ribera
Hisp.ˢ f.*
Provenance: General John Guise.
Literature: Bell, FF.31; Colvin, III, 33;
A. L. Mayer in Thieme-Becker, *Künst-
lerlexikon*, XXVIII, p. 233; the same,
Jusepe de Ribera, 1923, p. 210; E. Grad-
mann, *Spanische Meister-Zeichnungen*,
1939, No. 9; José Gomez Sicre, *Spanish*
Drawings, 1950, Pl. 34; W. Vitzthum
in *L'Oeuil*, Jan. 1963, p. 46.
Exhibited: Royal Academy, 1938, No.
473; Matthiesen, 1960, No. 64; Bowes
Museum, 1962, *Neapolitan Baroque*,
No. 8; Liverpool, 1964, No. 41.

One of the most important surviving drawings of the master, clearly drawn from the
model in the studio, and almost certainly a
study for St. Irene succoring St. Sebastian.
There is no correspondence with the painting of that subject dated 1628 in the Hermitage at Leningrad, but the fact that the
Hermitage painting is signed with the name
in precisely the same form might suggest a
connection. The same model appears as St.
Anne in the *Marriage of St. Catherine* in the
Metropolitan Museum, New York, which
is of 1643, fifteen years later than the painting at Leningrad; but there she looks older.

Illustrations

I. NICCOLÒ DELL'ABATE (?): Design for a Decorative Panel

2. ALESSANDRO ALGARDI: Design for an Altar (?)

3.   BACCIO BANDINELLI (?): A Camel

4. JACOPO DA PONTE, called BASSANO: Diana in the Clouds

5. ATTRIBUTED TO GIOVANNI BELLINI: Bust of a Man

6. ASCRIBED TO GIAN LORENZO BERNINI: Head of a Young Man

7. ANDREA BOSCOLI: A Stag-Hunt

8. GIACINTO BRANDI: S. Peter
Nolasco (?) Interceding with the
Virgin for Two Captives

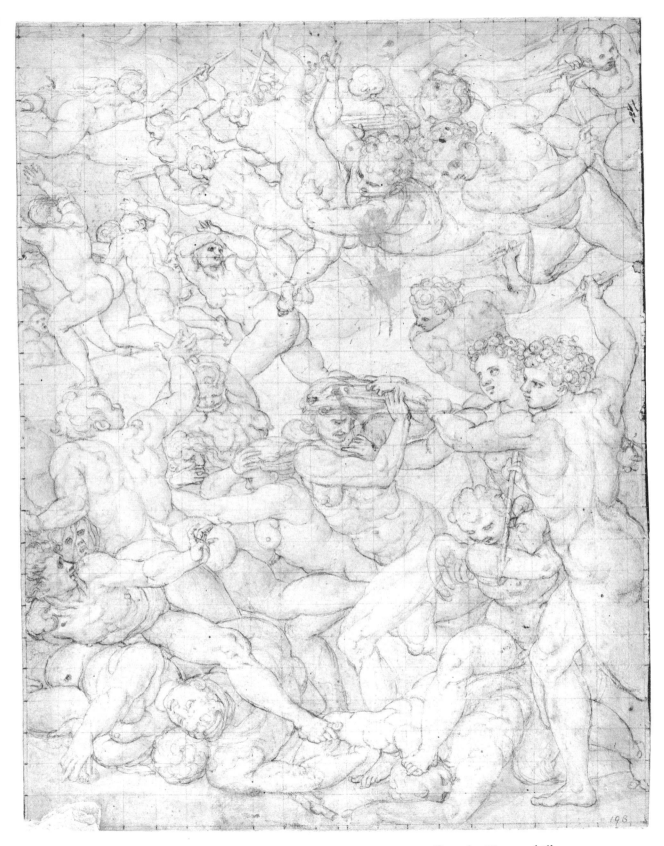

9. ANGELO BRONZINO: The Virtues and Blessings of Matrimony Expelling the Vices and Ills

10. DOMENICO CAMPAGNOLA: Mountain Landscape

11. SIMONE CANTARINI: The Virgin and Child, Seated

12. VITTORE CARPACCIO: Bust of a Young Man in a Cap

13. AGOSTINO CARRACCI: A Warrior Subduing a Monster

14. AGOSTINO CARRACCI: *Anchises*

15. ANNIBALE CARRACCI: A Male Nude Seated

16. LUDOVICO CARRACCI: Christ Shown to the People

17.   LUDOVICO CARDI, called CIGOLI: Studies for Two Celestial Virtues

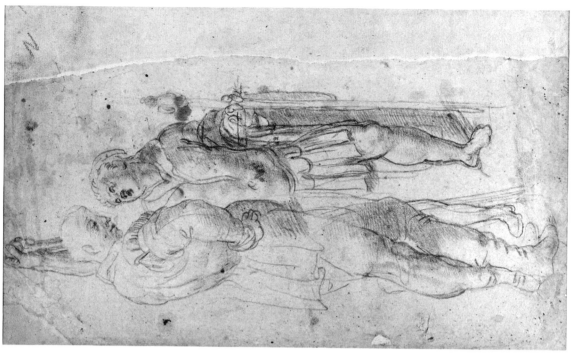

18. LUDOVICO CARDI, called CIGOLI: Two Soldiers Standing (verso)

18. LUDOVICO CARDI, called CIGOLI: A Soldier on Hands and Knees (recto)

19. JACOPO CONFORTINI: Christ in the House of Simon

20. CORREGGIO (ANTONIO ALLEGRI): The Virgin and Child with Saints and Angels

21. PIETRO DA CORTONA: Design for a Wall-Decoration

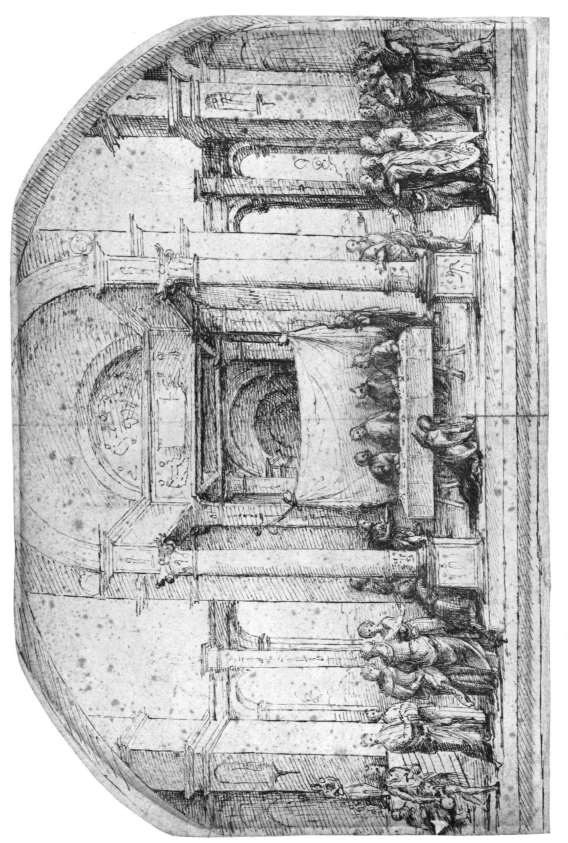

22. LORENZO COSTA: Christ in the House of Simon the Pharisee

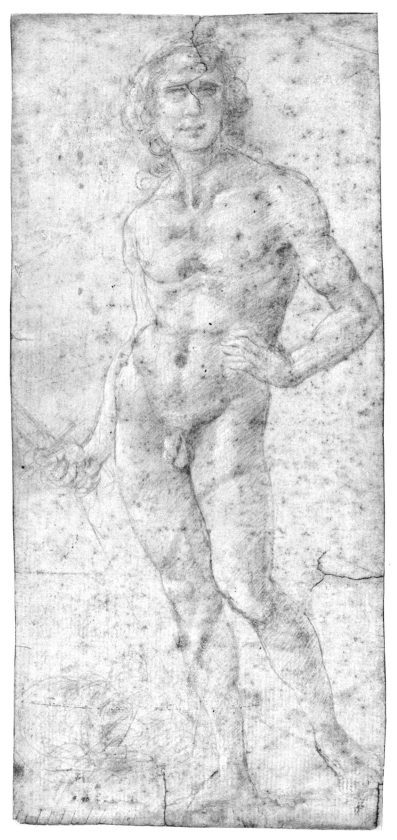

23. LORENZO DI CREDI:
David with the Head of
Goliath

26. PAOLO FARINATI: Apollo in His Chariot

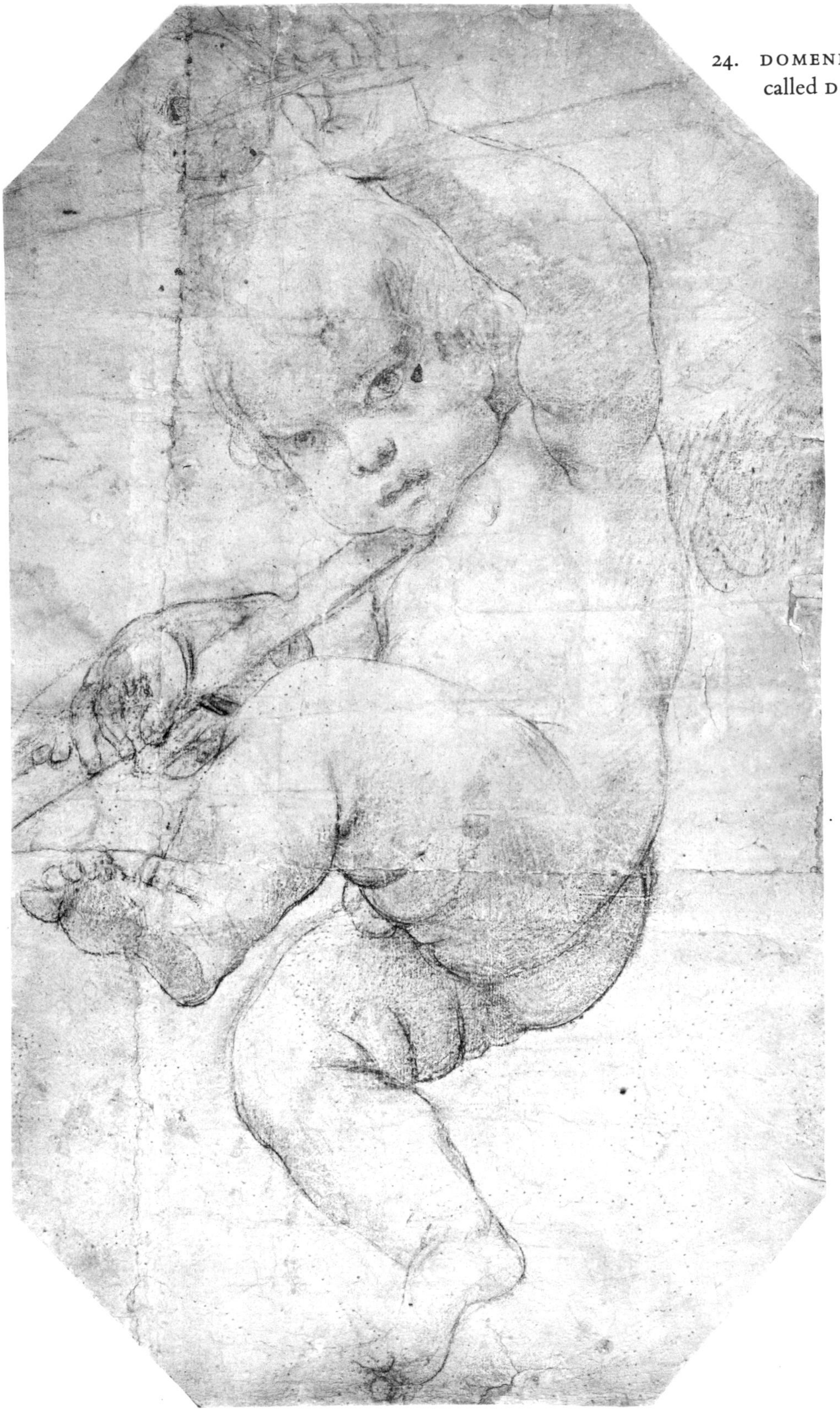

24. DOMENICO ZAMPIERI, called DOMENICHINO: A Flying Putto

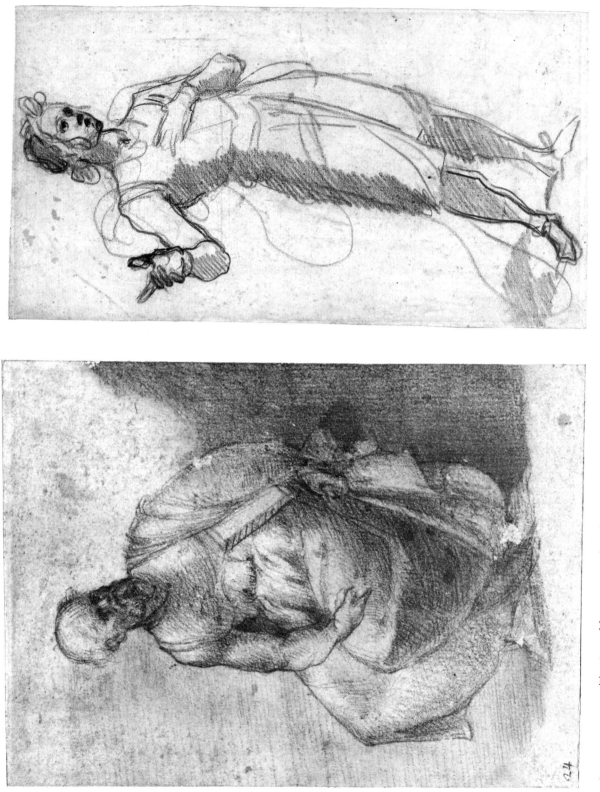

25. JACOPO DA EMPOLI: A Young Man Standing

28. GIORGIONE (?): An Old Man Seated with a Book under His Arm

29. GIULIO ROMANO: Design for a Gold Girdle

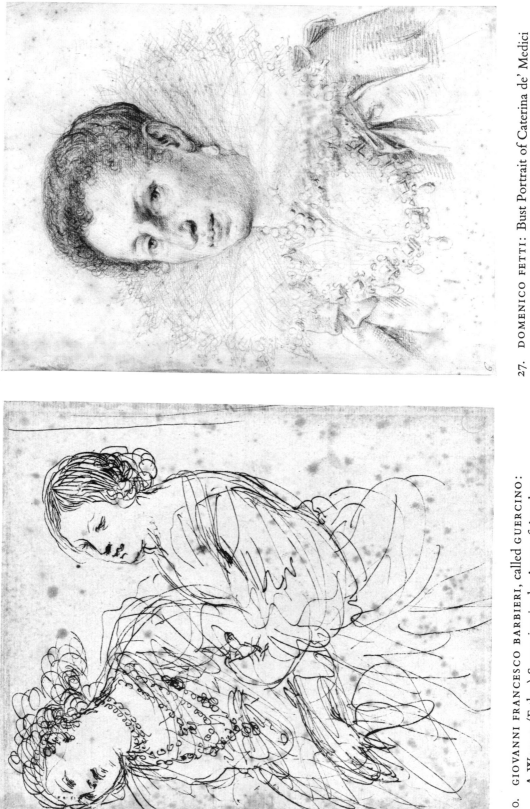

27. DOMENICO FETTI: Bust Portrait of Caterina de' Medici

30. GIOVANNI FRANCESCO BARBIERI, called GUERCINO:
A Woman (Esther) Swooning in the Arms of Another

31. GIOVANNI LANFRANCO: Head of a Young Man

32. GIOVANNI BATTISTA LENARDI: The Martyrdom of the *Quattro Coronati*

33. LEONARDO DA VINCI: Study of a Sleeve

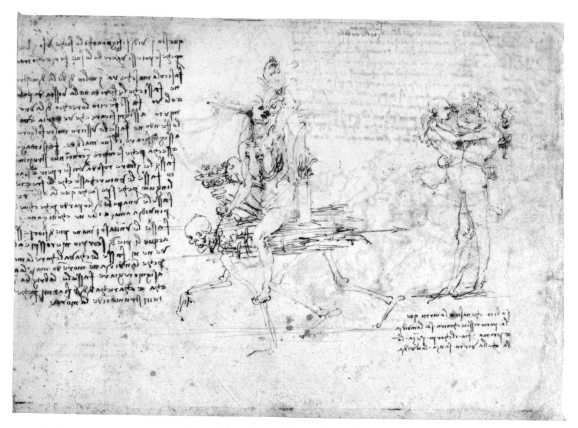

34. LEONARDO DA VINCI: Two Allegories of Envy (recto)

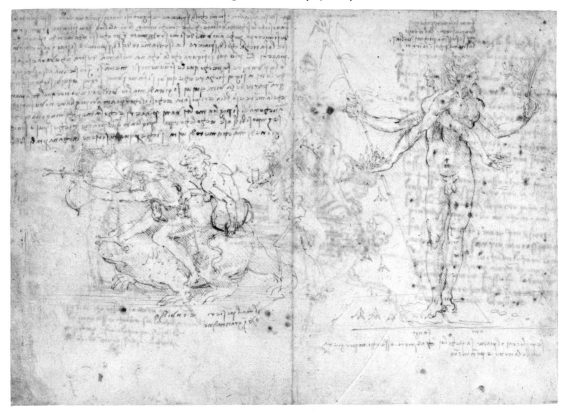

34. LEONARDO DA VINCI: Two Allegories—(a) Ingratitude, Envy, and Death;
(b) Pleasure and Pain (verso)

35. LEONARDO DA VINCI: Grotesque Bust of a Man

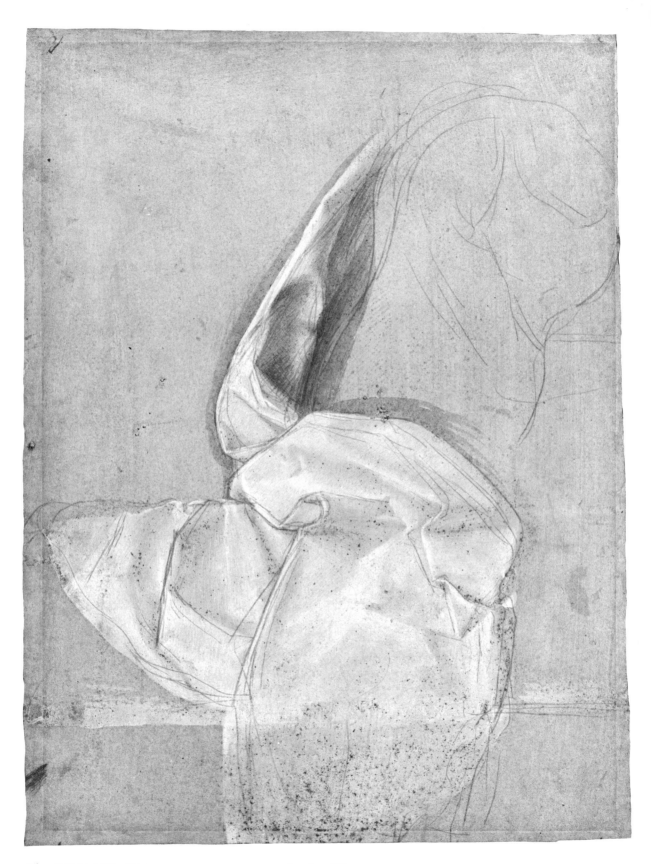

36. FOLLOWER OF LEONARDO DA VINCI: Study of Drapery

37. JACOPO LIGOZZI: Dante Watching the Sunrise in the Dark Forest

38. JACOPO LIGOZZI: Dante Surrounded by the Three Beasts

39. FILIPPINO LIPPI: A Page from Vasari's *Libro di Disegni*. Drapery of an Angel; Three Draped Figures; Two Draped and Two Nude Figures (recto)

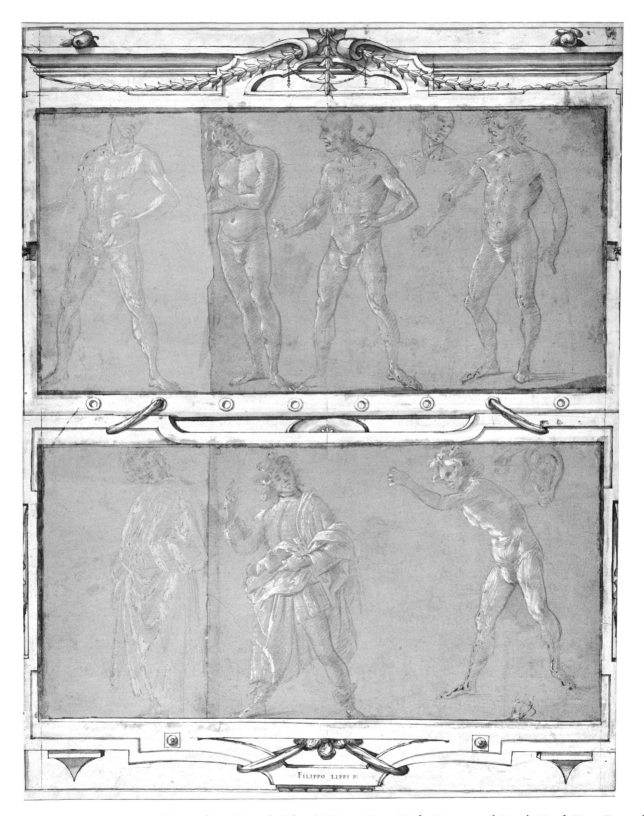

39. FILIPPINO LIPPI: A Page from Vasari's *Libro di Disegni*. Four Nude Figures and Man's Head; Two Draped and One Nude Figure (verso)

40. FILIPPINO LIPPI: A Page from Vasari's *Libro di Disegni*. Two larger drawings (A,B) and three smaller
(C,D,E) (recto)

40. FILIPPINO LIPPI: A Page from Vasari's *Libro di Disegni*. Design for an Altarpiece (attributed to "Altura Mantovano") (verso)

41. FILIPPINO LIPPI: A Man in Heavy Drapery

42. FILIPPINO LIPPI: A Litter-Bearer

43. LOMBARD SCHOOL: Study of a Young Man Wearing a Sword

44. STUDIO OF ANDREA MANTEGNA: Hercules and the Nemean Lion

49. PIER FRANCESCO MOLA: Two Children Playing with Rabbits

45. CARLO MARATTI: Self-Portrait

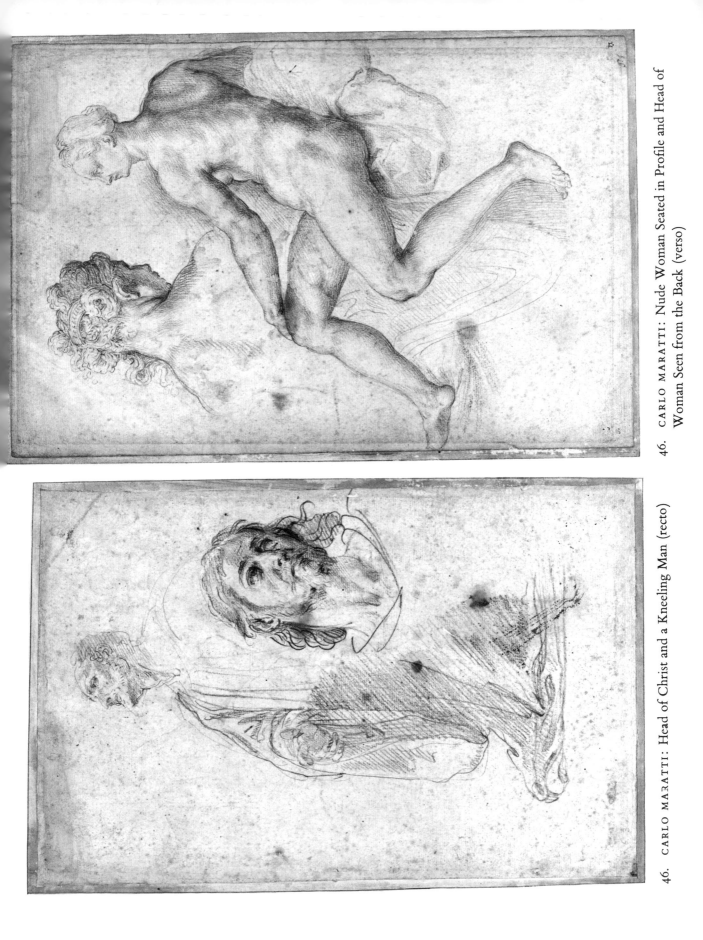

46. CARLO MARATTI: Nude Woman Seated in Profile and Head of
Woman Seen from the Back (verso)

46. CARLO MARATTI: Head of Christ and a Kneeling Man (recto)

47. MICHELANGELO: A Family Group (recto)

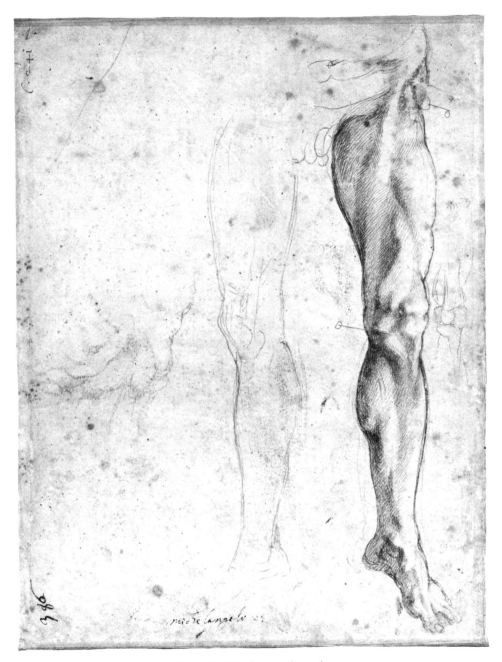

47. MICHELANGELO: Studies of a Man's Leg (verso)

48. MICHELANGELO: The Good Thief (?) on the Cross

50. LELIO ORSI: The Virgin and Child Seated in the Window Embrasure of a
Colonnade

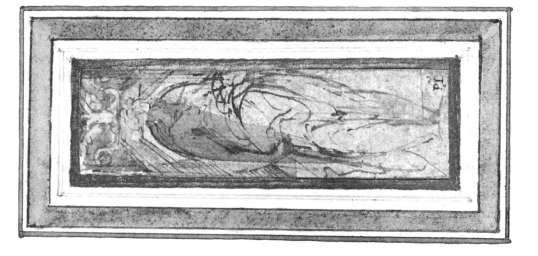

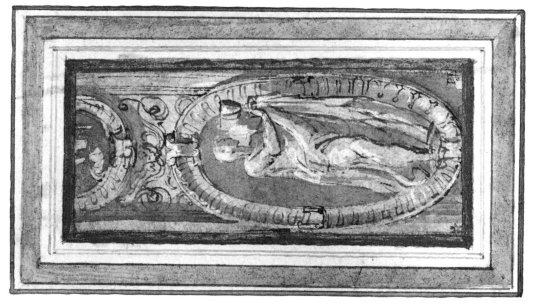

51. PARMIGIANINO (FRANCESCO MAZZOLA): Designs for Three Ornamental Panels

52. BARTOLOMMEO PASSAROTTI: Studies for the *Adoration of the Kings*

53. PIETRO PERUGINO: Bust of a Bearded Man

54. BALDASSARRE PERUZZI: An Allegory of Fortune

55. STUDIO OF ANTONIO PISANO, called PISANELLO: Head of a Pilgrim

56. POLIDORO DA CARAVAGGIO:
Studies for St. Jerome in Penitence

57. CESARE POLLINI: The Holy Family

58. JACOPO PONTORMO: The Deposition

59. RAFFAELLINO DEL GARBO: The Virgin and Child with S. Catherine and the Magdalen

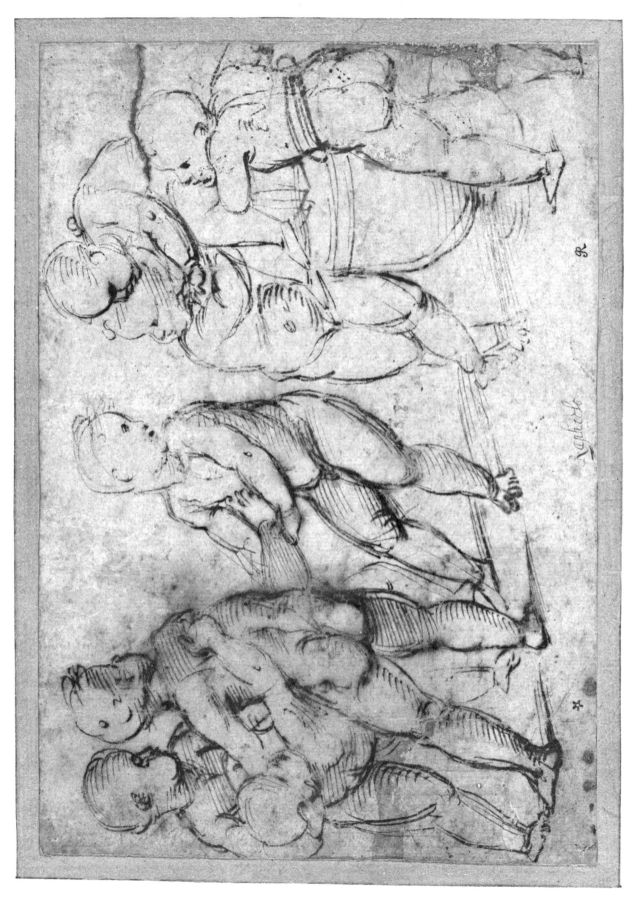

60. RAPHAEL: Seven Putti Playing

61. GUIDO RENI: Study for the Head of St. Proculus

63. GIOVANNI BATTISTA ROSSO (ROSSO FIORENTINO):
St. John the Baptist Preaching (?)

62. ROMAN (?) SCHOOL: Design for the Frieze of a Room

64. ROSSO FIORENTINO: An Ornamental Panel

65. FRANCESCO SALVIATI: Design for a Sacred Vessel

70. ANTONIO TEMPESTA: A Lion Hunt

66. FRANCESCO SALVIATI: Design for a
Clock

67. SEBASTIANO DEL PIOMBO: Study for the
Head of the Virgin Mary

68. ELISABETTA SIRANI: Self-Portrait

DI LEONARDO DA VINCI *Ritrato di Raffael d'Urbino*

69. GIOVANNI ANTONIO BAZZI, called SODOMA: Bust Portrait of a Young Man, Supposed to be Raphael

71. DOMENICO TINTORETTO: The Martyrdom of St. Stephen

72. JACOPO TINTORETTO: Head of Giuliano de' Medici

73. TITIAN (TIZIANO VECELLI): The Virgin and Child

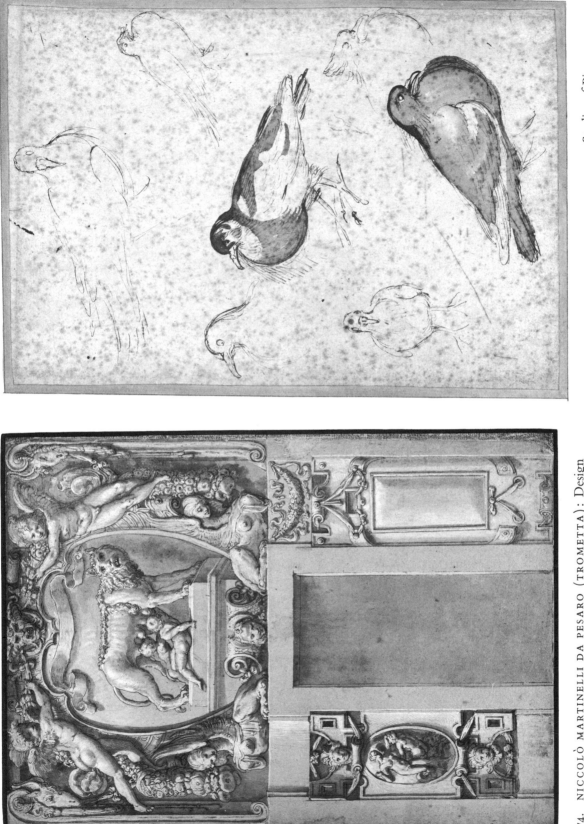

77. ASCRIBED TO GIOVANNI DA UDINE: Studies of Pigeons

74. NICCOLÒ MARTINELLI DA PESARO (TROMETTA): Design
for Part of the Decoration of a Façade

75. TUSCAN (?) SCHOOL: Three Apostles (?) Standing (recto)

75. TUSCAN (?) SCHOOL: Interior of a Gothic Chapel (verso)

76. TUSCAN SCHOOL: Bust of a Monk, Full Face

79. GIORGIO VASARI: Pope Leo X in Procession through Florence

80. GIORGIO VASARI: Duke Cosimo I and His Family

81. GIOVANNI DE' VECCHI: Christ in Glory with Saints

82. PAOLO VERONESE (PAOLO CALIARI): Sketches for the Coronation of the Virgin (recto)

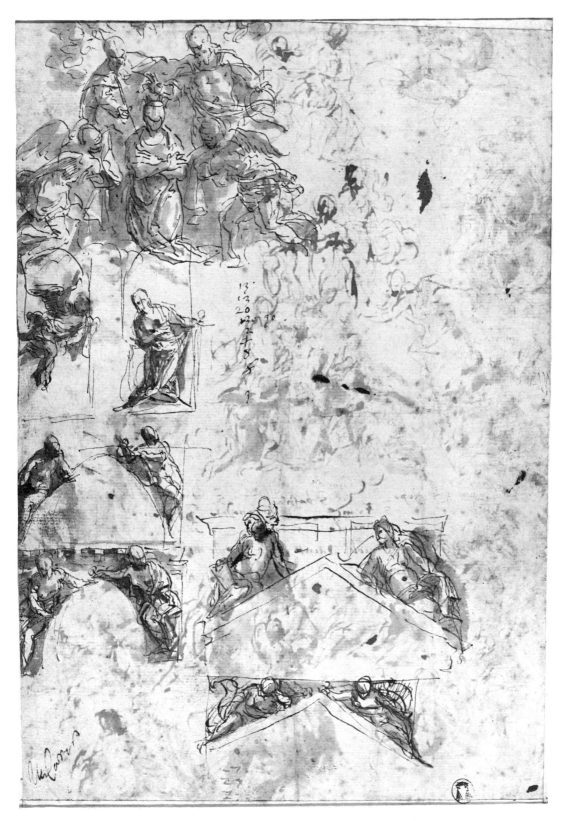

82. PAOLO VERONESE (PAOLO CALIARI): Further Sketches (verso)

83. PAOLO VERONESE: St. Dorothy

84. ANDREA DEL VERROCCHIO: Head of a Young Woman

85. FEDERICO ZUCCARO: Design for the Decoration of the Choir of the Cathedral of Florence

86. FEDERICO ZUCCARO: *Porta Virtutis*

87. TADDEO ZUCCARO: Study for an *Adoration of the Shepherds*

88. TADDEO ZUCCARO: Alexander and Bucephalus (recto)

88. TADDEO ZUCCARO: Sketches for a Basamento (verso)

89. JACOPO ZUCCHI: Design for a Chapel

ABRAHAM BLOEMAERT: The Mass of St. Gregory

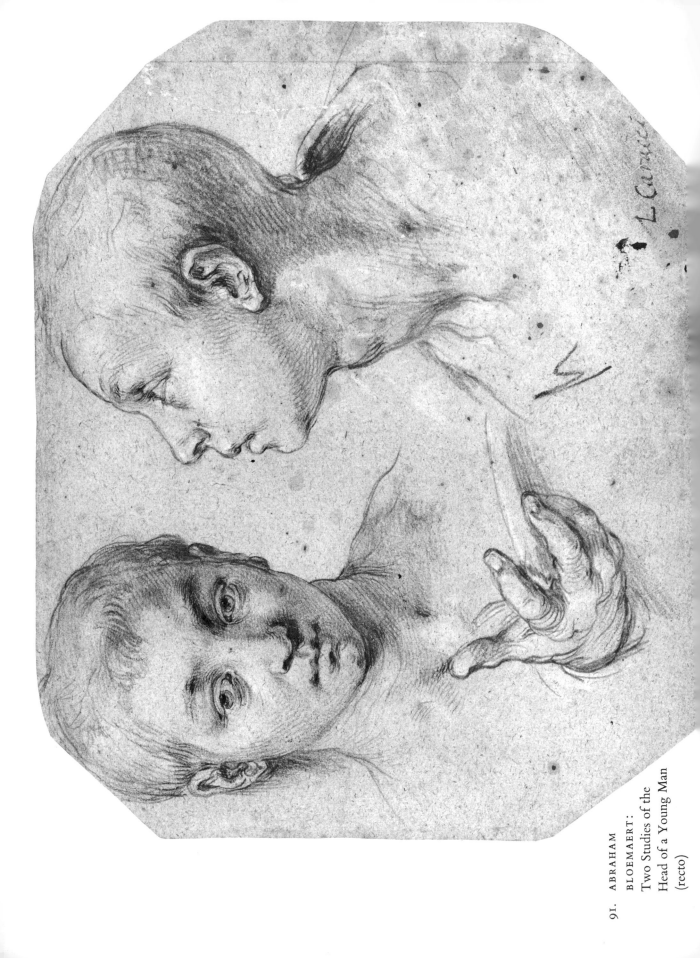

91. ABRAHAM
BLOEMAERT:
Two Studies of the
Head of a Young Man
(recto)

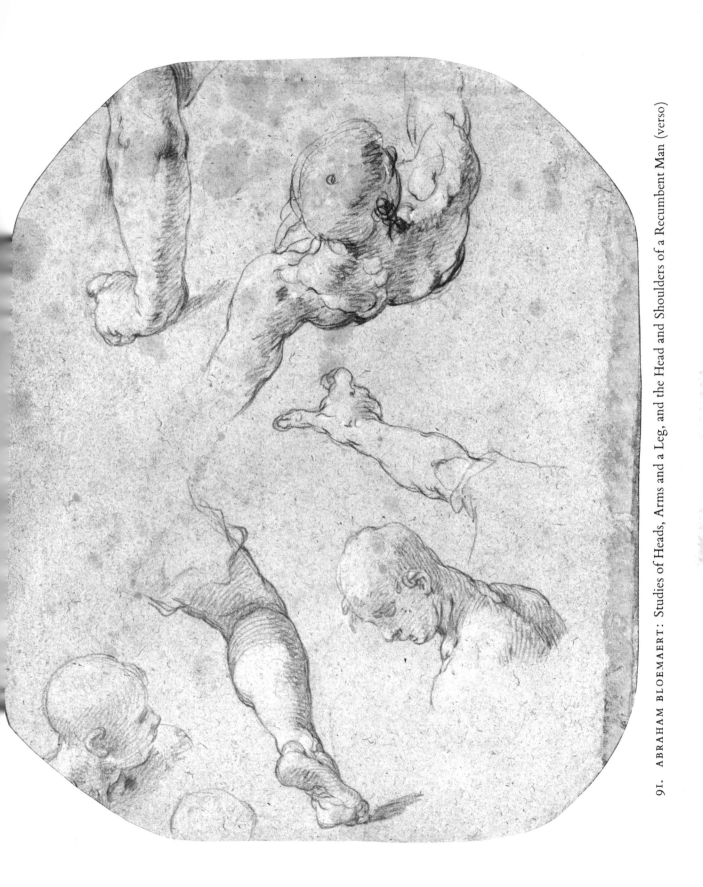

91. ABRAHAM BLOEMAERT: Studies of Heads, Arms and a Leg, and the Head and Shoulders of a Recumbent Man (verso)

92. ANTHONIE VAN BORSSOM: A Watermeadow with Cattle, on the Outskirts of a Town

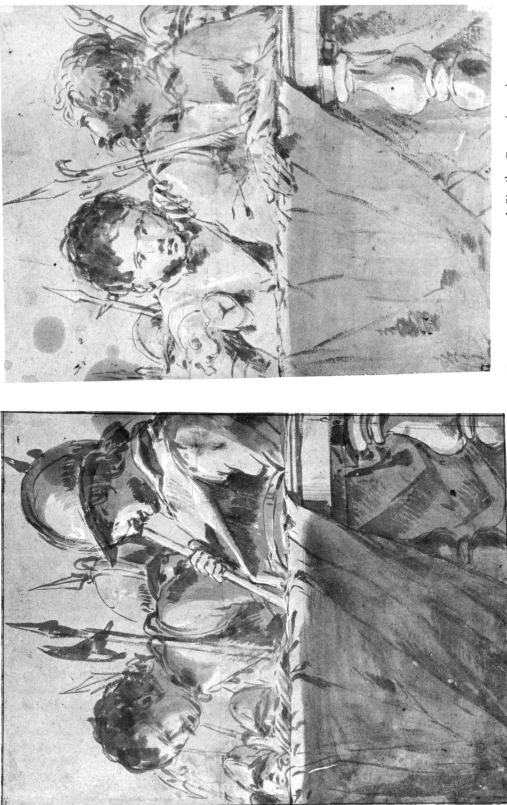

93. LEONARD BRAMER: A Similar Group (verso)

93. LEONARD BRAMER: Soldiers behind a Balustrade (recto)

94. BARTHOLOMÄUS BREENBERGH: Roman Ruins (the Baths of Caracalla?) (recto)

95. DUTCH SCHOOL: A Man Seated (Drawing?) on a Three-legged Stool (recto)

96. SIR ANTHONY VAN DYCK: Portrait of Justin van Meerstraten

97. JAKOB DE GHEYN II: A Witches' Sabbath

98. HUGO VAN DER GOES: Jacob and Rachael

99. JACOB JORDAENS: Bust of a Woman Wearing a Cap and Ruff

100. JAN LIEVENS: Farm Buildings among Trees

101. REMBRANDT VAN RIJN: A Nude Woman Kneeling on a Bed, Holding a Stick

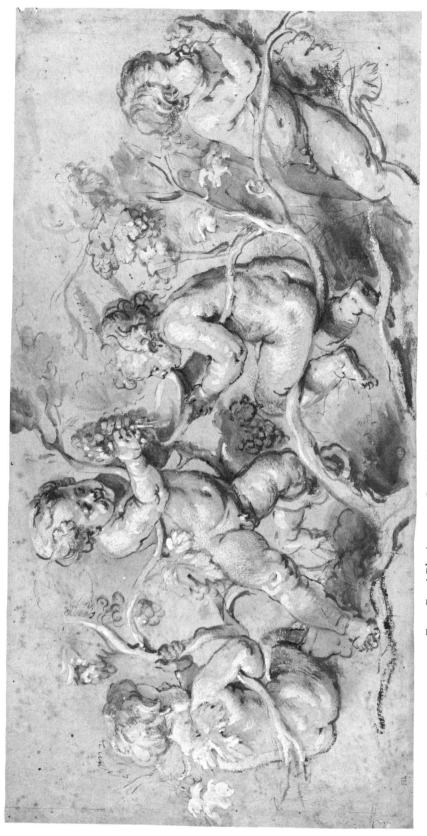

102. SIR PETER PAUL RUBENS: Four Putti Playing on a Grape-Vine

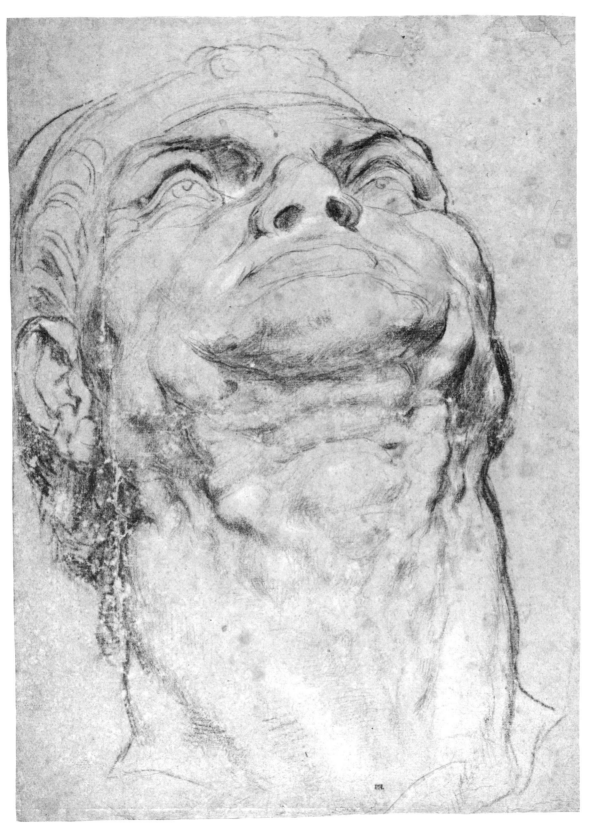

103. SIR PETER PAUL RUBENS: The Head of the Emperor Galba

104. SIR PETER PAUL RUBENS: Mars: Two Studies from a Sculptured Figure

105. ALBRECHT DÜRER: Study for the Tomb of a Knight and His Lady

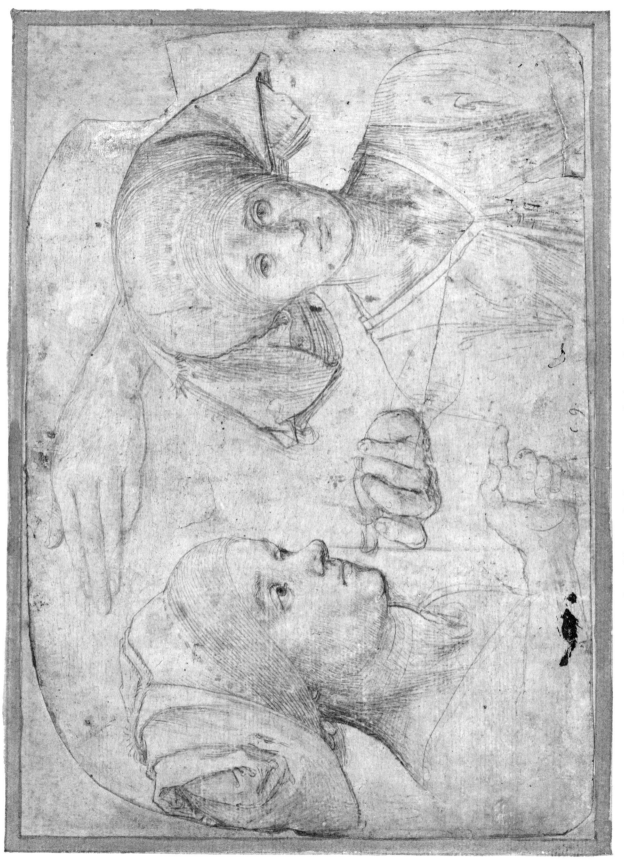

106. HANS HOLBEIN THE ELDER: Two Studies of the Head of a Woman, and Three of Hands

107. DANIEL LINDTMAYER: Design for a Glass-Painting

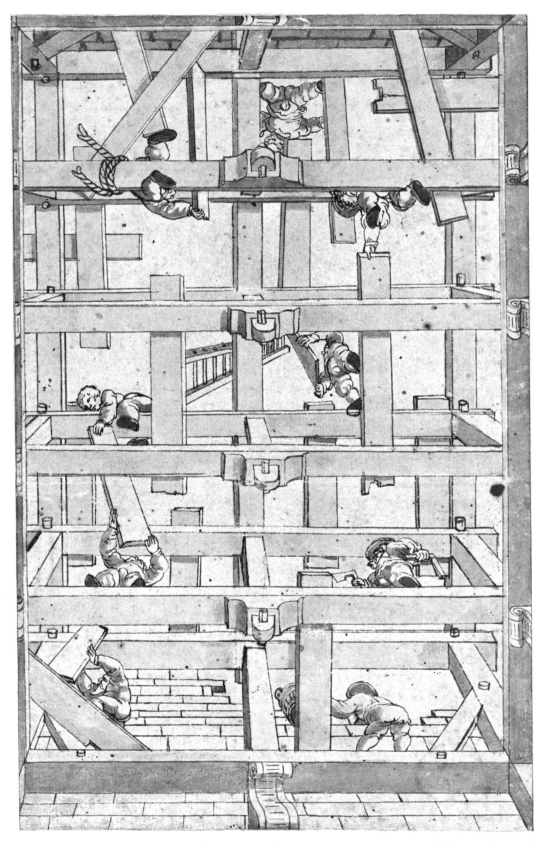

108. GEORG PENCZ: Design for an Illusionist Ceiling, Showing Workmen Building an Upper Storey

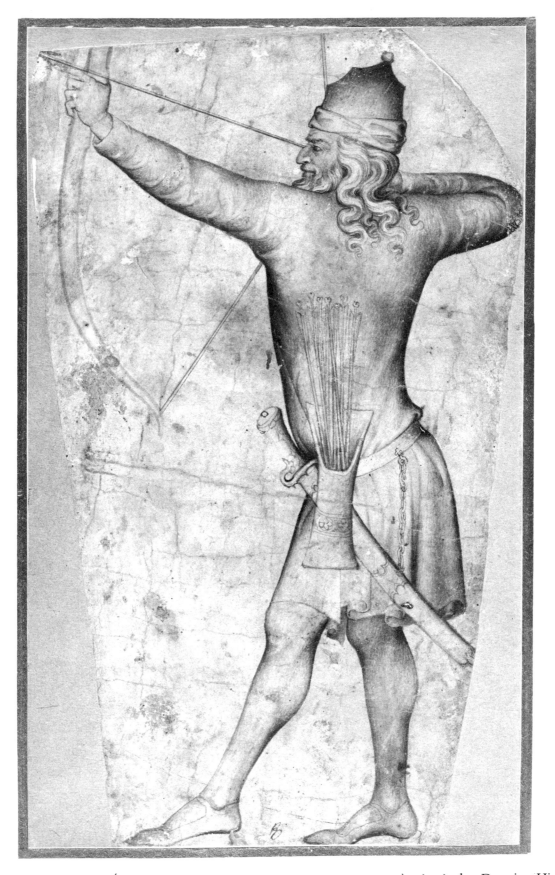

III. FRENCH SCHOOL (THE MASTER OF THE PAREMENT DE NARBONNE): An Archer Drawing His Bow

110. CLAUDE GELLÉE, called LE LORRAIN: A Group of Figures
Standing and Kneeling by an Altar (?) (verso)

109. CLAUDE GELLÉE, called LE LORRAIN: Rocky Landscape, with Two Large Trees, and a View of the Sea

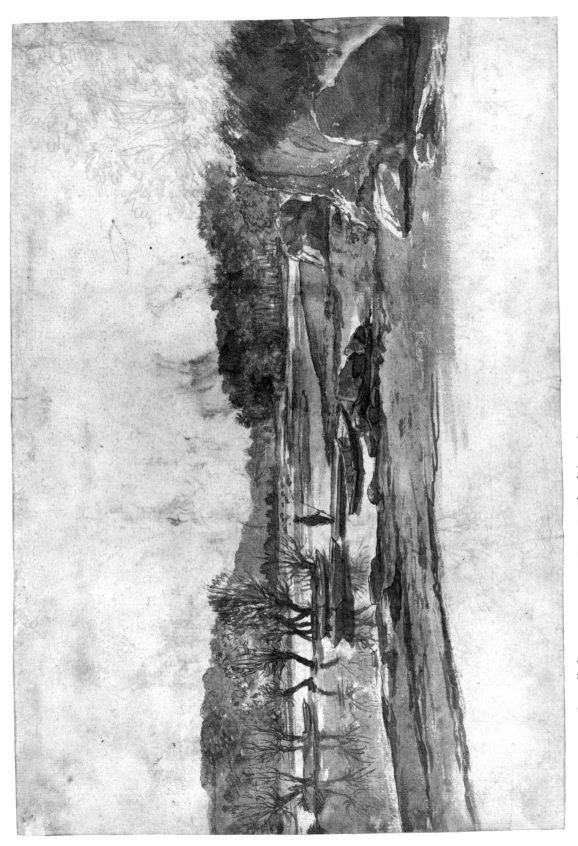

IIO. CLAUDE GELLÉE, called LE LORRAIN: A River in Flood (recto)

112. FOLLOWER OF NICOLAS POUSSIN: A View of S. Giorgio in Velabro, Rome

N. Poussin

113. FOLLOWER OF NICOLAS POUSSIN: A View of the Aventine Hill and the Tiber, Rome

114. FRANCIS BARLOW: Three Squirrels

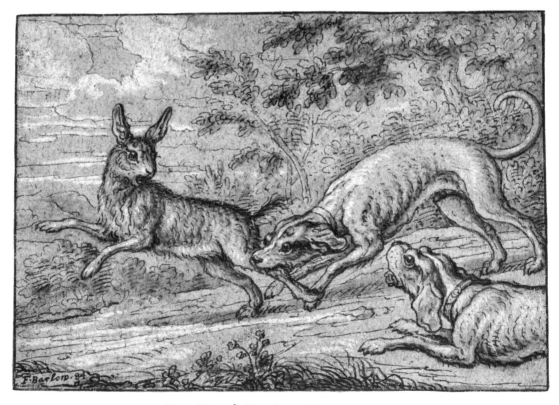

115. FRANCIS BARLOW: Two Hounds Hunting a Hare

117. INIGO JONES: Study of Three Male Heads

116. INIGO JONES: Studies of Heads, Legs and Torso of a Man

118. JUSEPE DE RIBERA: A Woman Looking Down